Table of contents

BASICS

MARKETING

Brian Sheehan

02

Online marketing

academia

An AVA Book

Published by AVA Publishing SA
Rue des Fontenailles 16
Case Postale
1000 Lausanne 6
Switzerland
Tel: +41 786 005 109
Email: enquiries@avabooks.com

Distributed by Thames & Hudson (ex-North America)
181a High Holborn
London WC1V 7QX
United Kingdom
Tel: +44 20 7845 5000
Fax: +44 20 7845 5055
Email: sales@thameshudson.co.uk
www.thamesandhudson.com

Distributed in the USA & Canada by:
Ingram Publisher Services Inc.
1 Ingram Blvd.
La Vergne TN 37086
USA
Tel: +1 866 400 5351
Fax: +1 800 838 1149
Email: customer.service@ingrampublisherservices.com

English Language Support Office
AVA Publishing (UK) Ltd.
Tel: +44 1903 204 455
Email: enquiries@avabooks.com

© AVA Publishing SA 2010

ISBN 978-2-940411-33-7

10 9 8 7 6 5 4 3 2 1

Design by David Shaw

Production by AVA Book Production Pte. Ltd., Singapore
Tel: +65 6334 8173
Fax: +65 6259 9830
Email: production@avabooks.com.sg

**Cadbury's 'gorilla'
viral advertisement**
Cadbury's Glass and a Half Full
Productions are offbeat, fun and
beg to be shared with friends –
the perfect recipe for a viral video.

>

Introduction

>

This book about the basics of online marketing has been a joy to write. What has made it so enjoyable is that online marketing is unquestionably the most dynamic and fast-moving field in marketing today. Considering that marketing itself is incredibly dynamic, it makes the subject of this book a very exciting one.

Before we dive into everything happening in the digital and online spaces, we need to take a quick step back. Specifically, we need to keep in mind that online marketing, while increasingly salient in our daily lives, is still a very young medium and still in its experimental stage. Online technology is continuing to improve in leaps and bounds. What looked incredibly cool and cutting edge just a few years ago now looks dated and quaint. Online marketing is changing form rapidly in an effort to keep up with technology, the speedy consumer adoption of new media, and new media ideas.

With things changing so quickly, a potential downside of a book like this is whether it will be relevant for very long. With this in mind, the book has been written with a focus on the major online trends that should continue in one form or another for a considerable time. It also highlights big marketing ideas and case studies that exemplify forward thinking, and which, I believe, can continue to inspire great online ideas well into the future.

The guiding principle of this book is a belief that every kind of marketing – offline or online, new or traditional – is all about ideas. At its best, marketing is about great ideas stimulating even better ideas. My friend and former colleague Bob Isherwood, who was worldwide creative director of the advertising agency giant Saatchi & Saatchi, liked to talk about our responsibility to create 'world-changing creative ideas'. From a marketing perspective, it is clear that we are only just beginning to realise the vast potential of the Web, which offers the best opportunities to create ideas that will change the world.

Chapter 1
The digital media revolution
Chapter 1 offers an introduction to the way that digital technology is changing media, consumers and marketers. We will also explore the digital media revolution, and examine the problems and opportunities that it has created for marketers.

Chapter 2
Search marketing
In Chapter 2 we will look at strategies for optimising results in both natural and paid search campaigns. The central importance of keywords and key phrases will be highlighted.

Chapter 3
E-commerce and e-branding
In Chapter 3 we will consider the two core business functions of the Web: selling products directly through e-commerce and selling products indirectly through e-branding.

Chapter 4
Advertising on the Web
In Chapter 4 we will explore the wide variety of advertising options that the Web provides. We will look at simple options (such as static banner ads), rich media options (such as Flash ads) and extended video options.

Chapter 5
The social web
In Chapter 5 we will look at how social networking is affecting online marketing. We will look at how online marketers are embracing a new reality which reaches beyond marketing to the masses or even to individuals.

Chapter 6
Online applications and mobile marketing
Downloadable applications are transforming both the computer industry and the mobile phone industry. In Chapter 6 we will consider how the Web is increasingly taking over the role of the computer's hard drive, giving rise to an explosion in online functionality.

Chapter 7
Measurement and analytics
Chapter 7 looks at the central role of analytics in online marketing. A key advantage of digital marketing is its inherent measurability. We will look at the importance of measurement reports, called 'dashboards', and the key performance indicators (KPIs) of which they are comprised.

Chapter 8
Ethical approaches
In Chapter 8 we will look at online marketing to children and how their online access requires marketers to protect children while trying to sell to them and/or their parents.

Broadband that keeps the whole family up to speed.

We're all demanding more from the internet, from live gaming, to streaming your favourite TV shows, to chatting online. So you need broadband that can cope. The power of our fibre optic broadband means the whole family can enjoy being online at the same time. It's enough to keep everyone happy.

0800 952 0856
virginmedia.com
visit Virgin Media stores

POWERFUL STU

**Virgin media –
the power of broadband**
As this advert from Virgin Media powerfully demonstrates, the accessibility of broadband Internet connections has changed the nature of media and given consumers an unprecedented amount of control over it.

This chapter provides important background information for each of the following chapters. It looks at the profound impact of the digital media revolution on marketing. First, it will define exactly what we mean by the 'digital revolution', by following its stages of development. We will then look at how this revolution has created new opportunities, and in some cases bigger problems, for marketers as the nature of media has changed.

In particular, we will look at how digital media has affected the expectations of consumers by giving them more control. We will then explore the ramifications of these newly empowered digital consumers. Consumer empowerment has led to a host of new approaches that are changing the fundamentals of marketing as well as how campaigns are integrated. We will end the chapter with a detailed case study of Telecom New Zealand, which used a unique combination of traditional, online and mobile media to achieve big success.

What is the digital revolution?

To begin to tackle the subject of online marketing, we must look first at the fundamental changes that have led to its sudden appearance and rapid growth. Online marketing is an offshoot of advances in digital technology, which occasioned the birth of the Internet, the World Wide Web and interactive media. The development of the Internet as a communications medium has been through a number of stages. The most notable stages are commonly called Web 1.0 and Web 2.0.

Web 1.0 and 2.0

Web 1.0 and 2.0 are notional, made-up terms, marketing terms if you will; therefore, their definitions can vary considerably. Technologists tend to define the difference between the two based on advances in the capability of online production technologies and the proliferation of their use due to decreasing costs.

For marketers, however, Web 1.0 is usually seen as a narrow and relatively static communications medium. Early websites were structured using Hyper Text Markup Language (HTML), allowing people to download information and contact the marketers if desired. They sometimes had the appearance of interactivity but in reality were mostly linear, one-way communications.

Web 2.0 was marked by the emergence of real interactivity on the Web. Aided by the advent of consumer-friendly browsers and powerful search engines, the ability to find, view and interact with websites became fast and easy. New programming technologies enabled constant and continuous feedback between marketers and consumers at every stage of the online process. They also allowed consumers to manipulate content on websites and to contribute their ideas to them.

Perhaps the most significant recent development for marketing on the Web has been the emergence of interactivity *between* users. Social networks, e-communities, and social networking features of marketing websites have connected millions of consumers around the world with each other.

The Semantic Web is not a separate Web but an extension of the current one, in which information is given well-defined meaning, better enabling computers and people to work in cooperation.

Tim Berners-Lee
British engineer, computer scientist
and MIT professor

Some marketers argue that the social web defines a new stage in the Internet's history, or Web 3.0. However, technologists argue that Web 3.0 will be ushered in by computers using artificial intelligence to read web pages, and to search through them in the same way that people do. Tim Berners-Lee, the man credited with inventing the World Wide Web, terms this the 'Semantic Web'.

Regardless of how its history or future is defined, the emergence of the Internet has profoundly altered the marketing landscape. Specifically, it has introduced interactivity between marketers and users, as well as between single users and other users.

Interactivity creates both big opportunities and potential problems for marketers. It helps marketers to foster relationships at a level never before possible in traditional media such as television and magazines. Interactivity allows them to have a continuous conversation with the people buying or interested consuming in their products. But with opportunity also comes complexity.

Noise

In any communications model, a marketer's message can be impacted by **noise**. Noise obscures marketing messages. It can be created by such things as advertising clutter, consumer inattention, or negative publicity about a marketer's product. For example, if an oil company is running advertising at the same time that an oil spill is being reported, the message may be ignored, misunderstood, or even create exactly the opposite reaction to that intended.

A primary cause of noise is consumer confusion about the marketing message. Nothing interferes with a message more than the recipient having a hard time understanding it once it gets through the clutter. Marketers spend lots of money researching messages to make sure that confusion and miscommunications are kept to a minimum. Noise is a particular problem for marketing online, because the interaction and ongoing communication between consumer and marketer is often continuous. Continuous dialogue increases the chances of miscommunication, and one miscommunication can easily create another and so lead to increased frustration.

Running glossary

noise
anything that interferes with the marketing message communicated to the intended receiver

Buzz

The introduction of social networking features on the Web has also created a new type of noise for marketers. While marketers are having continuous conversations with their consumers, their consumers are having conversations with networks of like-minded people. When these social conversations between consumers are about your product, it is called **buzz**. Buzz can either be positive or negative. Monitoring and influencing buzz are key aspects of online marketing.

In a nutshell, marketing online is more complicated and challenging than marketing offline ever was. On a more positive note, it can also be far more rewarding when done well.

Traditional and interactive communications models

The traditional communications model is simple and linear, but external noise created by advertising clutter, consumer inattention, or negative publicity can interfere with the message being communicated properly. The interactive communications model has even more potential for consumers and companies to misinterpret information due to increased amounts of noise as messages go back and forth.

>

Running glossary

buzz
online social discussion between consumers about your product or service

Traditional communications model

| Sender | Noise → | Channel | Noise → | Receiver |

Interactive communications model

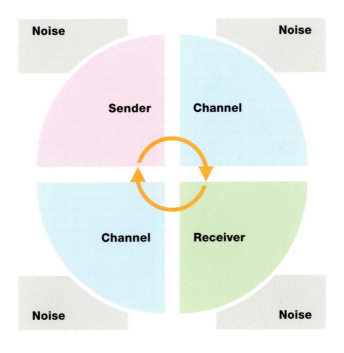

Noise

Noise

Sender

Channel

Channel

Receiver

Noise

Noise

Beyond the emergence of the Internet, the digital revolution is fundamentally changing traditional media. On a surface level, traditional media have had to change their production and transmission processes. Television and radio now have digital signals. Newspapers and magazines today use digital photography and reproduction. It has become quite common to see digital outdoor billboards. *Esquire* magazine's 75th anniversary issue even used an electronic digital cover that flashed versions of the message: 'The 21st Century Begins Now'. Similarly, Pepsi and CBS network ran a print ad in *Entertainment Weekly* that had a small screen, which played video montages of existing shows, ads for Pepsi and sneak peeks of new shows at the touch of a button.

Traditional media are being challenged to intrinsically reinvent themselves, while online media are being challenged to deliver the levels of emotional engagement that traditional media like television have always achieved. In fact, traditional media is beginning to look a lot more like online media and vice versa. Importantly, new hybrid media and technologies are also being developed that bridge the gap between 'old' and 'new' media.

Television

Television is changing rapidly. The advent of personal video recorders (PVR), such as those available from Sky TV in Europe and TiVo in the US, has wreaked havoc with television programming schedules. PVRs record your favourite shows, storing them as digital memory, so that viewers can watch their favourite shows whenever they want, not just when they are broadcast. This is known as **time shifting**. In 2009, in the United States, penetration of PVRs grew to about 30% of all households and time shifting was up 40%.[1] Additionally, a large majority of those who time shifted watched the programming without commercials.

These developments have led to significant changes in television programming. Time shifting has changed the long-held concept of 'prime time', or so-called 'appointment viewing'. Lower advert viewership due to time shifting has also led to a reduction in advertising revenue, which in turn means that there is less money available for TV show production. Therefore, scripted programming is declining in relation to reality programming, which is cheaper to produce.

Running glossary

time shifting
using a personal video recording device (PVR) to watch a TV programme at the time of your choosing, rather than when it is actually broadcast

Susan Boyle demonstrates YouTube's tremendous reach

YouTube is a popular 'channel' with global reach. Susan Boyle became a worldwide phenomenon when her performance on *Britain's Got Talent* was posted onto YouTube.

Esquire's electronic digital cover

Digital technology is bringing exciting changes to traditional media. For example, *Esquire* magazine used a digital cover for its 75th anniversary issue.

‹ What is the digital revolution?
How has the digital revolution changed media?
› How has the digital revolution affected consumers?

Online alternatives

Traditional TV viewership has also been assailed by popular web-based video programming. The most prominent and popular web-based alternative to television is YouTube. An evening in front of YouTube can be just as entertaining as an evening in front of the TV. You can watch it at your leisure, and you can share what you like with friends. According to the web traffic-monitoring site <alexa.com>, YouTube is the third most visited site on the Web, worldwide. In countries as far-flung as Albania, Germany, Iran or Brazil, YouTube is a top website. Unlike television channels, however, YouTube does not have a subscription or advertising revenue model, so its ability to make a solid long-term profit is still questionable.

Video sites such as YouTube, which do not create their own content, are presented with some unique challenges, such as protecting copyrights for content uploaded by users. In Italy, in early 2010, three Google executives were found guilty *in absentia* and sentenced to six months in jail for invasion of privacy. The case was initiated when a group of students uploaded a video clip showing them bullying a classmate with Down's Syndrome. Although Google removed the clip immediately it was discovered, the executives were still found culpable.

TV programming is also being augmented by hybrid models that combine traditional TV programming and online access. Hulu is a good example.

Hulu is an online channel that allows people to watch quality first-run programming online. The lure of a successful online channel is so attractive to TV programmers that Hollywood heavyweights such as Disney's ABC, NBC Universal and Fox have all invested in Hulu and made programming available to it.

Other developments in cross-platform programming availability include Apple TV, a device that allows digital online content to be viewed on high-definition TV sets (HDTV). Slingbox, on the other hand, is a device that allows people to view their television programming from their computers.

Television programming is now coming to the Web, and web-inspired features like on-demand programming have become mainstays on cable and satellite TV. In the near future, it will be hard to decide where television ends and the Internet begins. Kevin Roberts, author of *SiSoMo: The Future on Screen*, has noted that differences in programming are increasingly about which screen you decide to view it on. Increasingly, similar content will be available on your mobile phone, your computer and your television. The only difference will be a question of where it is most convenient, and relevant, for you to view it. This ability for many digital devices to run the same basic media software is a key aspect of media convergence.

The convergence of television and online media can also be seen in the growth of video on the Web, which is currently growing at 13% year on year.

The Daily Beast offers an alternative to print newspapers
Many consumers are turning to websites in place of traditional print media. Websites such as <thedailybeast.com> combine features of traditional newspapers and magazines with digital delivery and functionality.

Radio

Radio has also benefited from the effects of digitisation. For example, satellite radio with hundreds of digital narrowcast stations has become a standard feature in many new cars. In fact, in 2006, one of America's most popular and controversial radio personalities, Howard Stern, left terrestrial radio for satellite radio provider Sirius, which brought lots of attention and listeners to the new radio delivery system. By 2009, however, Sirius was on the verge of bankruptcy, sharing the fate of many new digital media providers, underscoring the need for new digital media companies to find profitable business models.

< What is the digital revolution?
How has the digital revolution changed media?
> How has the digital revolution affected consumers?

Print

Traditional newspapers have been affected financially more than any other medium by digital competitors. Ready access to a plethora of news content websites has doomed many long-standing newspaper brands. Large circulation US newspapers such as the *Seattle Post-Intelligencer*, *Rocky Mountain News*, and the *Christian Science Monitor* have either shuttered their businesses completely or stopped producing print editions to take their chances with an online publishing format that has yet to prove its profitability. The problem is global. For example, Britain's Trinity-Mirror Group folded nine regional papers in 2009, having already closed 27 newspapers and sold four others in the previous year.

Traditional newspapers have been replaced not only by online news sites but also by sites such as *The Daily Beast*, which was started by Tina Brown erstwhile editor of such magazines as Britain's *Tatler*, *Vanity Fair* and *The New Yorker*. *The Daily Beast* leads with breaking news, but also includes entertainment news, fashion, gossip, blogs and social networking.

Magazine readership is also down, as consumers have many lifestyle content options available on the Web. However, for the best magazine brands, the outlook is significantly brighter. Strong brands with clear value propositions, such as *Vogue* magazine, have had the chance to extend their brands into new digital media while maintaining a large print audience. As David Carey, group president of *Vogue*'s publisher Condé-Nast puts it, 'When we have a print offering combined with a digital offering, that's ideal.'

Outdoor

Perhaps nowhere has the digital revolution led to more of a transformation than in the outdoor advertising medium. Static printed posters are increasingly being replaced by giant digital screens that bring sight, sound, motion and emotion to a once bland platform. The static boards that do remain have to be extremely creative just to get noticed. This situation has led to a renaissance of creativity in outdoor media. Hybrid examples also exist, where traditional print boards feature two-dimensional barcodes or other interactive features, which can interact with mobile phones or electronic cards to download various types of content. In Japan, for example, over 28 million passenger train cards are in circulation, which use radio frequency identification (RFID) that can interact with platform posters offering information, prizes, discounts and so on.

Media fragmentation

One of the most significant effects of the digital revolution has been the **fragmentation** of media. Where there was once only a handful of major channels, magazines or newspapers, there are now hundreds of channels and millions of websites. Fragmentation of media has in turn led to the fragmentation of audience, making it harder for any individual channel, programme or story to attract a mass audience. However, there are still exceptions. In the US, for example, the Super Bowl still commands a huge premium from advertisers ($3 million/£2 million per spot in 2009). It is one of the few places where a large audience tunes in to one programme all at once.

The opposing forces of fragmentation and convergence, happening concurrently, are a key reason why today's digital media landscape is so hard for marketers to navigate.

MINI's interactive outdoor advertisement
Interactive billboards using radio frequency identification (RFID), such as this one for MINI, can trigger personalised messages, instant information and discounts to consumers when they are out and about.

Running glossary

fragmentation
the proliferation of specialised digital media channels that has led to the division of viewing audiences into smaller, fragmented groups

The digital revolution has done more than offer new choices in media. It has also significantly changed consumer behaviour. One of the most fundamental ways that it has changed consumers is in their ability to adapt to new technology. As a consequence of these changes, one of the cornerstones of modern marketing – the consumer adoption curve – is now being directly challenged.

The consumer adoption curve

The consumer adoption curve describes how people approach new products or technologies. According to this theoretical model, when a new option becomes available to consumers, a small number of mavericks or 'innovators' (who represent less than 3% of the population) will try the new product or technology. They are willing to take a risk to be on the cutting edge. Innovators are then followed by 'early adopters'. These are people who want to be in on new things before they hit it big with the masses. They see themselves as trendsetters. Once these two groups have bought in, the majority of the public will then follow them and buy in too. Seventy per cent of people will be in either the 'early majority' or the 'late majority'. At the end of the curve are the 'laggards'. These are the people who buy in long after almost everyone else has. Some people never buy in. For example, my mother is in her 80s. She has never had a computer and she never wants one.

The adoption curve has been an institution in marketing for decades. It has been a constant in a sea of change. For most products, progress through the curve has been measured in years. For technologies, it was often measured in ten years or more.

Like everything else in marketing, however, the digital revolution is also changing the way that consumers adopt new technology. An instructive example here is the iPod. According to the curve, consumers should have taken many years to adopt iPods and other MP3 music players. Instead, they were adopted very quickly. Within a few short years of the launch of the hand-held iPod, a large chunk of the population owned one, a much larger chunk than predicted by the curve. Now, almost everyone has an iPod or an MP3 player. To date, over 200 million have been sold worldwide.

In the case of the iPod, the curve was shortened and flattened. But why? The reason is that as consumers adopt new digital technologies they get better at it and more comfortable doing it. This leads to the acceleration of adoption. Sometimes, in fact, consumers are ready for a new product or technology *before* it becomes available.

The consumer adoption curve

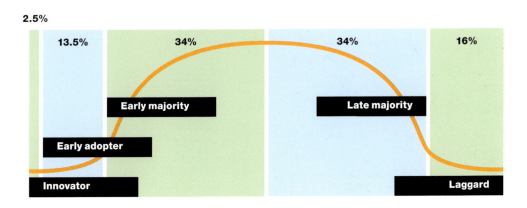

2.5%

13.5%   34%   34%   16%

Early majority   Late majority

Early adopter

Innovator   Laggard

In the case of the iPod, people didn't say, 'What is that thing and how does it work?' They said, 'Fantastic, I've been waiting for something like that.' The combination of new digital technology and easy digital downloading software (such as iTunes), was irresistible to consumers – almost all consumers, all at once.

In his bestselling book, *The Tipping Point*, Malcolm Gladwell posits that adoption of new things can spread like viruses. In other words, small changes in a system can lead to big effects, in a way akin to contagion. Digital technology has passed the tipping point and has become second nature in consumers' daily lives.

The consumer adoption curve
The consumer adoption curve has for years described the process by which consumers embrace new products and technology over relatively long periods of time. A small group of innovators and early adopters set the trend and are followed later by the majority of customers. However, the digital revolution has changed the way that consumers adopt technology, shortening and flattening the curve.

⟨ How has the digital revolution changed media?
How has the digital revolution affected consumers?
⟩ Case study: Telecom New Zealand adopt a multimedia approach

Product research and purchase

Digital technology has also changed how consumers research and buy products. While online shopping has not met the exaggerated predictions of the early dot.com days, that it would put bricks-and-mortar stores out of business, it is still a significant and worldwide phenomenon. According to a 2008 Nielsen research report,[2] less than 20% of the world's population had shopped online. However, looking solely at the world's online population the number was an astounding 85%! Large industrial economies such as those of Japan, South Korea, the United Kingdom, the United States and Germany were all 94% or above.

The Internet has reshaped the way that people buy highly priced items, such as automobiles, even when the product is eventually bought in a physical store. Not that long ago, the starting point for purchasing a car was a trip to a few dealerships to collect brochures that contained all the product specifications and prices. This first trip often started the negotiation process with the salesman.

Today, car buyers gather all the information they need on the Internet before they even think about stepping into a showroom. Manufacturers' sites, auto-information sites (such as <edmunds.com> and Kelley Blue Book, <kbb.com>), auto-buying sites (such as <cars.com>), car magazine sites, car blogs and so on, all allow customers to research, build, price and compare cars at home. By the time the customer gets to the dealership, he or she is ready to buy. They know what car they want, what they want from it, and what price they should be paying for it. Automotive brochures are now largely useless, except as a nice souvenir of the car you have already bought. This process has taken a tremendous amount of power out of the hands of auto-dealers and salespeople and put it right into the hands of the consumer.

Running glossary

prosumers

consumers who actively engage in product development and/or marketing concept development by means of online open source software

It's a story about community and collaboration on a scale never seen before. It's about the cosmic compendium of knowledge Wikipedia and the million-channel people's network YouTube and the online metropolis MySpace. It's about the many wresting power from the few and helping one another for nothing and how that will not only change the world, but also change the way the world changes.

Lev Grossman
Time magazine's lead technology writer commenting on *Time* magazine's 'You' Person of the Year cover

The empowered consumer

Digital technology has changed the balance of power in marketing. In fact, it has begun to reverse it. Consumers have a lot more control. Increasingly, they manage the purchasing process, as well as the marketing messages they see. They even participate in the development of products they want to see in the future.

The emergence of consumer power in the marketing process was recognised by *Time* magazine, when they announced that the 2006 *Time* Person of the Year was 'You'. Time chose all of us instead of one of us because the World Wide Web had allowed the many to wrest power from the few. In the context of marketing, the 'many' are everyday consumers and the 'few' are marketers.

In the marketing realm, consumer control has had other profound effects. One of the most important has been that of consumers' desire to be involved in product and creative development. No longer willing to sit on the sidelines and be presented to, people are getting involved in the creation of the marketing message itself. Consumers are now also collaborators. Marketers have come to call this growing segment of the population '**prosumers**' because they actively influence production and consumption. Consumer collaboration in advertising messaging led *Advertising Age* magazine to follow in a vein similar to Time magazine. In 2007 they named 'The Consumer' their Agency of the Year.

< How has the digital revolution changed media?
How has the digital revolution affected consumers?
> Case study: Telecom New Zealand adopt a multimedia approach

Consumer collaboration: Diet Coke and Mentos

One of the cases *Advertising Age* cited as evidence of consumers as effective advertisers was the runaway success of a consumer-produced video called 'The Diet Coke and Mentos Experiment'. The video, which was produced without the involvement of either Diet Coke or Mentos and was distributed on a video-sharing website called <revver.com>, showed two men in lab coats performing an experiment by dropping Mentos mints into bottles of Diet Coke. The ensuing chemical reaction resulted in gushing streams of soda. With a little showbiz flair, the men made elaborate, synchronised, Vegas-style fountains of soda. The popularity of the films led to a 15% increase in sales of Mentos! All of this happened without a marketing professional in sight.

At first, the brands did not necessarily approve of unauthorised people broadcasting films about their products. However, once they saw the huge popularity of the experiments, they partnered with the men in question (Fritz Grobe and Stephen Voltz), and their nascent website/film production company EepyBird Productions, to conduct more experiments. EepyBird has now been hired to produce films for other clients, such as Office Max and ABC television. In the digital age the line between enthusiastic prosumer and professional content creator is a very thin one.

Doritos

Consumer-generated marketing is big business. In 2010, for the fourth year in a row, PepsiCo ran a 'Crash the Super Bowl' campaign for their Doritos brand, where an advert contributed by a consumer would be run on one of the world's most expensive media placements: the Super Bowl. Spots in the Super Bowl can cost $2 million to $3 million, and Doritos offered an additional $1 million prize if the advert was voted the number one spot on the Super Bowl by the closely watched *USA Today* Ad Meter. The finalist was chosen from over 2,000 consumer film entries.

> A brand has only ever been as good as consumers' experience of it. The difference today is that consumers have lots of ways of communicating those experiences, and trust each other's views above marketers' overt sales pitches. Consequently, they're influencing marketing strategy as never before.
>
> Matthew Creamer
> Senior Editor
> *Advertising Age*

<Eepybird.com>:
The Diet Coke and Mentos
experiment
The Diet Coke and Mentos
experiment videos were created
by consumers, but proved very
successful in promoting the
brands involved. This kind of
unofficial content exemplifies
the blurring of lines between
brand-generated communication
and consumer-generated
communication.

The distinctions between producers
and users of content have faded into
comparative insignificance.

Axel Bruns
Queensland University of Technology,
Australia

⟨ How has the digital revolution changed media?
How has the digital revolution affected consumers?
⟩ Case study: Telecom New Zealand adopt a multimedia approach

The Lexus mosaic

The Lexus mosaic was an interesting example of co-creation that mixed elements of the Web and outdoor media to launch the Lexus IS 300 sports sedan. The campaign focused around a website where consumers could upload their favourite pictures, which were then combined with over 100,000 other consumer-generated photographs to make a photo-mosaic picture of the new IS 300. When you visited the site and put in your information, the site would zoom into the picture of the car to see exactly which part of the car included your pictures. This could be shared with friends on the Web.

The Mosaic site was connected to the giant Reuters electronic board in Times Square, New York, where passers-by would see the photo of the car and then zoom in to see the different pictures that made it up. Every person who contributed their photos to the site had their pictures featured on the giant Times Square board.

Lexus' Times Square mosaic billboard

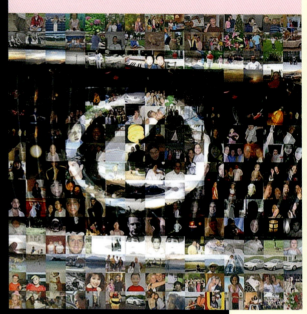

To add to the excitement, Lexus had street teams taking pictures of people in Times Square and instantly posting their photos up to the mosaic. In the end, many people were taking pictures of their own pictures on the billboard in Times Square to e-mail back to their friends and family.

Lexus attracted 600,000 visitors to the site. Around 70,000 people uploaded photographs. And 45,000 asked for more information about the new IS 300.

How has the digital revolution changed marketing?

The relationship between marketing and the Web has been a rocky one. In the late 1990s, and the early part of the next decade, dot.com hyperbole and over-investment in flimsy online commerce ideas led to the dot.com bubble bursting. By the mid-2000s marketers started to embrace online marketing as being worthwhile in its own right, albeit in a cautious and experimental fashion. In the last few years, online marketing has been taken seriously and begun to hit its stride.

In 2008, despite the onset of a financial crisis that led to a double-digit drop in total US advertising spending, online ad spending was up over 10%. Internet advertising revenue did dip 3% in 2009, but this was still far less than other media.[3] And it still has a lot of growth left. For example, Procter & Gamble, the world's largest advertiser, has been estimated to spend less than 10% of their advertising budget online.[4]

Marketers have started to embrace digital media. Perhaps more importantly, they have gone beyond stand alone online websites and begun to integrate their online marketing with their offline marketing.

For example, as we've just seen, Lexus used online marketing in conjunction with outdoor media, while Doritos used it in conjunction with TV. This is just a start. Marketers are now challenging themselves to develop true **integrated marketing communications** (IMC), which presents a holistic view of marketing that does not differentiate between online and offline marketing, but rather sees them both as equal parts of a complete communications approach.

Running glossary

integrated marketing communications (IMC)
a planning process designed to ensure that all brand contacts received by a customer or prospect for a product, service or organisation are relevant to that person and consistent over time [5]

〈 How has the digital revolution affected consumers?
Case study: Telecom New Zealand adopt a multimedia approach
〉 Questions and exercises

In 2006, Telecom New Zealand (TNZ) took full advantage of prosumers and their desire for co-creation with the launch of their new video-capable mobile phones. Their business challenge was to engage the youth market. The youth market is critical to the mobile phone industry because of its size and readiness to adapt to new technologies. For Telecom New Zealand, the youth market was even more important because their research showed that New Zealander 'twenty-somethings' had a fixed view of the company as being old and very businesslike; not young, or fun.

To capture the imagination of younger people and to get them to rethink their image of TNZ, they created Rubbish Films, the world's first mobile phone film festival. The goal of the festival was to encourage people to make and send video clips via their new high-speed T3G mobile network. They had a strong advantage over their competition as the only New Zealand network operating with 3G speed (3G stands for 'third generation' of mobile telecommunications standards, which was first launched in Japan in 2001). TNZ could now provide tech-savvy youth with an experience they could not get anywhere else. However, they only had a narrow window of three months before competitors entered the market with a similar product.

The campaign's cheeky tone of voice, combined with technology that enabled young people to express themselves and share cool films with their friends, proved irresistible. TNZ was able to zero in because they did a lot of research to understand the motivations of New Zealand's youth. They gave them the moniker 'Generation C' because:

■ they wanted to express their *creativity*
■ they wanted to produce their own *content*
■ they wanted to be in *control*
■ they wanted their own level of *celebrity*

Integrated marketing communications

Beyond taking advantage of consumers' desire to be prosumers, TNZ positioned online marketing as the centrepiece of an integrated marketing communications campaign. They used video-based media, including television commercials on youth-oriented programmes and music channels, as well as banner ads, to drive people to the website. The website was the hub of the campaign. It was the place to upload video entries and to view other entries. Website visitors even voted online to choose the eventual winner. The winner received an all-expenses-paid trip to… where else? Hollywood.

TNZ surrounded the site with blogs. They created fake rival sites. They even handed out phones to encourage video shoots at youth events. Television, the Web, mobile, events, promotions – this campaign coordinated them all to drive participation and website traffic.

Throughout the campaign, TNZ stayed true to their goal of enabling youth in an authentic fashion. Their TV commercial was even made by local film students. As TNZ and their advertising agency stated it in their summary of the campaign, the results showed that: 'The Rubbish Film Festival created a genuinely rewarding experience for the cynical youth market and one they were prepared to pay for.' TNZ executed the entire campaign in all media for under $500,000, far less than the budget for typical launch campaigns.[6]

The results

The campaign garnered 71% awareness of Rubbish Films by young New Zealanders. Within three days, the site was one of the top five websites in the country with over 400,000 page hits. It had 1,000,000 visits during the campaign period, not bad for a country with only 4,000,000 people. Around 900 films were entered during a four-week period.

The Communications Association of New Zealand gave the campaign its gold award for advertising effectiveness in 2006.

The Rubbish Film Festival… demonstrated a brave move by Telecom New Zealand to take a critical look at what it wanted to achieve and endorse the radical approach suggested by the agency [Saatchi and Saatchi].

Brian Weaver
Convener of the Effie Awards' judges

‹ How has the digital revolution affected consumers?
Case study: Telecom New Zealand adopt a multimedia approach
› Questions and exercises

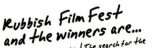

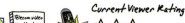

Question 1
If you worked on a brand that was trying to reach out to the youth market, what other types of digital media might you use to reach them?

Question 2
Would there be other creative ways to showcase the speed of the 3G mobile network online, aside from a mobile movie festival?

Rubbish Films Festival
Telecom New Zealand's 'Rubbish Films' was the world's first mobile phone film festival. The campaign adopted a multimedia approach that centred on a website where films could be uploaded, downloaded and voted upon. This campaign, exploiting developments in phone technology, allowed TNZ to reach the youth market that had previously eluded them.

Questions and exercises

>

Discussion questions

1

How has your behaviour changed due to advances in digital technology in the last three to five years?

2

If you were planning to buy a car or take an expensive vacation this year, how would you use the Internet to take control of the purchase and how much you finally pay for it?

3

What do you think the impact will be of empowered consumers on the profitability and staffing of product marketing companies such as Procter & Gamble and Unilever?

Exercises

1

Draw the consumer adoption curve. Make a list of products that you bought and where on the curve you were when you bought them. Are you consistently in one place (e.g. an early adopter) or are you in different places depending on the product?

2

Break into groups. Your job is to create a new product that will take advantage of accelerated consumer adoption. What kind of product will you create? What are people already waiting for? Compare the plans for the different groups.

3

How might you leverage consumer collaboration to launch a new product or revitalise an old one? List five ways by which you might achieve this. Remember, consumers can help with product design as well as with communication.

Summary

This chapter has examined the fundamental changes in marketing resulting from the digital communications revolution. Specifically, it has focused on the emergence of online marketing as the most salient of the new media platforms. Throughout the rest of the book we will continue to look at online marketing through various lenses, but we will begin with one of the most fundamental tools: search.

Suggested further reading

Gladwell, M. 2001. *The Tipping Point: How Little Things Can Make a Big Difference.* New York: Abacus

Garfield, B. 2009. *The Chaos Scenario: Amid the Ruins of Mass Media, the Choice for Business is Stark: Listen or Perish.* New York: Stielstra Publishing

Useful websites

<www.shellypalmermedia.com>

<www.navigatenewmedia.com>

Endnotes

1
Shields, M (29 May 2009). 'TV viewing, time-shifting rise'. *Mediaweek*. Retrieved from <www.hollywoodreporter.com> (28 May 2009)

2
'Over 875 million consumers have shopped online…' (28 January 2010). Retrieved from <www.nielsen.com> (15 July 2009)

3
IAB Internet Advertising Report: 2009 full year results (April 2010). Retrieved from <www.iab.net> (10 April 2010)

4
TNS media intelligence/NYT (19 November 2008)

5
American Marketing Association. Retrieved from <www.websitemarketingplan.com> (10 April 2010)

6
Saatchi & Saatchi NZ

Ask Jeeves:
Search has evolved
As this striking advert from Ask
Jeeves states, search engines
are evolving to meet the needs
of an increasingly demanding
online audience. Search is where
everything starts on the Web. It
is the foundation of all successful
online marketing.

This chapter looks at search marketing
as the cornerstone of online marketing.
We will explore the two key types of
search marketing: natural search and
paid search. We will explore the vital role
played by 'key words', and come to
understand the importance of a strategic
approach to improving search results,
known as search-engine optimisation (SEO).

We will learn that search marketing is all
about consumers requesting information,
which creates unique challenges for
marketers who are used to pushing
information onto consumers directly. We
will also see that search engines are still in
a very rudimentary stage and that they are
poised for significant, if not radical, change.
We will explore the evolution of search
engines with a case study examining
Microsoft's challenge to Google with their
search engine called 'Bing'.

Is search really considered marketing?

Is search really considered marketing? It is a fair question. To most people, search is just a way to find things on the Web, not something that they consider to be marketing, like a promotion, a TV commercial or an online display ad. To marketers, however, search is one of the *most* important aspects of modern marketing. Arguably, it is now the most important aspect.

Search is media. In fact, search dominates online media spending. In 2009, search was the largest single advertising revenue generator on the Web. It accounted for 47% of all online advertising revenue, as opposed to 22% for online display advertising and 10% for classified ads. Lead generation and e-mail advertising accounted for the rest.[1]

Over 90% of people use search to launch websites, whether they know the URL address or not.[2] If you are a marketer and you want to generate traffic to your website for direct online sales or branding, knowing how to optimise your search results is an absolute must. In today's digital media environment, a good search marketing strategy can mean the difference between brand success or brand failure. It can safely be said that most online marketing begins with search.

It is not enough to have your product just show up in the search results; you must also make sure it is consistently listed in the top results. If your product does not appear on the first page of the results or even above the results that need to be scrolled to see (in other words 'above the fold') there is very little chance that a significant number of people will visit your site. Sixty-two per cent of searchers don't go beyond the first page.[3] You can build a fantastic site, but people need to find you easily. If they cannot, your site, your brand and your product will consistently underperform online.

✕ Punching above your weight

In their book *Watch This, Listen Up, Click Here*, David Verklin and Bernice Kanner profiled a small US company that exploited search engines to outperform bigger, more established players. Aubuchon, a chain of 135 neighbourhood hardware stores in New England, popped up fourth from the top when 'hardware store' was typed into Google. How did it beat bigger, national players like Sears and Lowe's? Aubuchon had a search-engine optimisation (SEO) programme that it followed consistently and relentlessly.

Natural search, keywords and search optimisation

Search marketing is broken into two basic areas: *natural search* and *paid search*.

Natural search (also called 'organic search') is a free function of search-engine providers like Google and Yahoo!. The search engine, which works using a complex mathematical algorithm, lists results based on the perceived relevance of the website, or web page, to the search terms inputted by the person who started the search. Search engines figuratively 'crawl' the Web looking for relevant websites. The crawling mechanisms are known as 'spiders'. Spiders find relevant sites by matching keywords found on sites with the keywords used in the original search, as well as by matching keywords to relevant links to and from the site.

Because natural search is essentially free to marketers, there is much to be gained by increasing the ability of your site to be found by the search-engine spiders. Being judged as relevant to as many keywords as possible that consumers use to find your product, or product category, can be the difference between success and failure on the Web. For example, if you run a department store, you will want your brand to appear whenever anyone types your store's name or a generic descriptor, like 'department store'. You will also want it to appear when people type words like 'luggage', or 'underwear', or 'fashion' and so on into a search engine.

In fact, no matter what business you are in, you probably need to be deemed relevant to dozens, hundreds or even thousands of search words or phrases. Insurance companies, for example, need to be linked to obvious words and phrases like 'insurance', 'insurance companies', 'rate quotes' and 'coverage for my house'. But they also need to be linked to less obvious ones like 'wind', 'storm', 'broken window', 'leaks' and many, many more.

This free connection to your target, when they are actively looking for what you provide, is the most efficient marketing possible. With so much potential business on the line, companies have begun employing significant resources and scientific approaches to improve their natural-search results. This process is called search-engine optimisation (SEO).

According to <marketingexperiments.com>, some tips for optimising natural search include:

■ Choosing the right keywords and phrases that offer potential for significant traffic

■ Focusing specific site pages on specific keywords

■ Giving relevant names to your site's pages

■ Submitting your site to as many specialised directories as possible to create as many relevant links to your site as possible, making it easier for spiders to find

Google results for 'laptops' – paid and natural

In this example for the search query 'laptops', Dell appears near the top on natural search and paid search listings. Competitors like Apple and HP also appear further down in the paid listings, but don't match Dell's dominance in the natural listings. Having strategies to optimise both natural and paid search is vital. Strength in one without strength in the other can be a big competitive disadvantage.

Paid search

Paid search is just that. It is a guaranteed place or rotation on the search results page based on marketers paying for that placement. We've already seen that search advertising is the largest source of advertising revenue on the Web; paid search is where the money comes from. According to ZenithOptimedia, while overall advertising spending in all media will be down 12.9% in 2009, online advertising will be up 14.1%. According to their report, the 'most growth will come from paid search'.

Paid search listings sit side by side with natural listings, usually in shaded boxes above and beside the natural results, labelled 'sponsored links'. Google, the world's largest and most successful search engine, sells these positions (also called 'search ads') for keywords or phrases based on an auction. In order to ensure that inferior sites do not just pay more to get the top listing, Google awards the positions based both on the amount of money bid for them and their relevance as judged by links to other relevant sites. This helps Google maintain the quality of their results and avoid disgruntled users who might otherwise click on top 'paid' results and not find what they are looking for.

Cost per click

Search ads are usually sold on a cost-per-click (CPC) basis, meaning that the advertiser pays the search engine the amount of money it bid to get the position every time someone clicks on it. Depending on the competition for the keyword or key phrase, the cost can be extremely cheap or extremely expensive per click. The cost for some words can get truly astronomical when marketers feel they will lead to high-value customers. Words related to expensive medicines and medical procedures command high prices. For example, it was reported in September 2009 that the word 'Mesothelioma' (a rare form of cancer) sold for almost $100/£62 per click.

<marketingexperiments.com> has outlined the following tips for optimising the click-through on paid ads: realise that the title copy is the most important element; use relevant keywords in the title copy; list prices in the title if they are competitive; use the shortest website address possible (because even when people don't click on your ad this increases the branding potential for later use).

Paid search is important to marketers because it guarantees a certain level of search visibility and performance. However, success in natural search is perhaps even more important. In addition to its lower cost, natural search has many other advantages over paid search. Natural search results have higher click rates – 70% of people choose organic listings first.[4] Also, consumers judge the value of paid listings based on the natural ones they see below it.[5] Natural listings lend credibility to paid ones.

Click fraud

Online advertising, whether through search ads or display ads, is prone to a unique type of abuse from competitors, or online mischief-makers, called click fraud. Because marketers usually pay money every time someone clicks on their ads, the ads can be exploited by computer programs that click on them continually. By clicking on the ads on a continuous basis, they run up the cost for marketers, either to gain competitive advantage or just to create havoc. Search-engine companies must discount or rebate a significant amount of their fees to advertisers to account for click fraud.

Click fraud has been estimated as making up between 15% and 26% of all clicks.[6] One survey by Radar Research even claimed that half of all online advertising impressions and 95% of all clicks were potentially fraudulent. The cost of click fraud is huge. According to Steve O'Brien, Vice President of Marketing at Click Forensics, '[Click fraud] could be as high as $4.35 billion [£2.9 billion] if none of the fraud were detected. In Vietnam, for example, one out of every two clicks was registered as click fraud.'

Click fraud can also lead to lawsuits. In 2009, a sports website called RootZoo sued Facebook, alleging that on a given day there were only 300 clicks generated by Facebook, when they were charged for 804.

From marketing push to consumer pull
⟩ Case study: Google versus Bing

In many ways, search has ushered in a complete revolution in marketing. For the best part of a century marketing has been about producers of products and services finding customers or 'markets' for their products. Today, search engines allow consumers to initiate the marketing process and control it in a way never before possible.

Historically, the marketing process was initiated by marketers, and imposed on consumers, via tools such as advertising. As consumers watched, listened or read various programmes or articles, they were exposed to marketing messages. Consumers did not choose which messages they would see. In fact, they had no idea what they would be seeing until they saw it. Now, search allows consumers to 'pull' marketing messages, whereas in the past, marketing messages were 'pushed' to them by marketers. Search has allowed *consumer intent* to be a trigger for marketing messages.

A short history lesson

Modern marketing is a direct result of the Industrial Revolution. During this period, particularly when it hit full stride in the late 1800s, factories were able to produce goods on an unprecedented scale. For the first time in history, the ability to provide goods and services far outstripped demand. This created tremendous competition to find buyers, or 'markets', to buy those goods. Marketing, as we know it today, was created to deal with this excess of supply over demand. For example, Ivory Soap, arguably the first true consumer brand in the United States, was an offshoot of the production increases driven by the Industrial Revolution combined with the demand increases created by the Civil War.

Analogue world: Approximate number of daily exposures to adverts

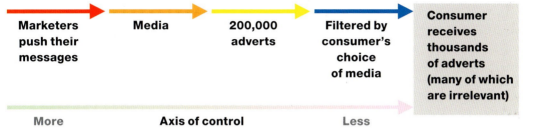

Marketers push their messages → **Media** → **200,000 adverts** → **Filtered by consumer's choice of media** → **Consumer receives thousands of adverts (many of which are irrelevant)**

More — Axis of control — Less

Digital world: Approximate number of daily exposures to adverts

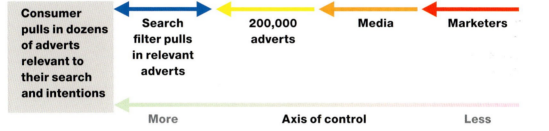

Consumer pulls in dozens of adverts relevant to their search and intentions ← **Search filter pulls in relevant adverts** ← **200,000 adverts** ← **Media** ← **Marketers**

More — Axis of control — Less

Analogue and digital worlds: Daily exposure to adverts

In the analogue world, marketers 'push' messages to consumers and many get through. The consumer is a blind receiver. However, in the digital world, consumers increasingly request specific information with a more limited number of adverts attached to it. The consumer is an active receiver.

< Is search really considered marketing?
From marketing push to consumer pull
> Case study: Google versus Bing

Consumer intent as a starting point

Consumer intent as the starting point of brand communication is not just another example of customer empowerment. It is a transformation of the relationship between the marketing messages consumers see and the perceived relevance of that information. Search marketing messages are highly relevant to a degree that other messages can rarely be. This is a win-win situation. Consumers get relevant information when they want it. Marketers with ads placed highly on the results page get their messages in front of consumers at the exact moment when that information can most influence an immediate or eventual sale.

Search as a filter

One way to look at search is as a filter. In the past, consumers could only filter advertising messages based on choosing one TV channel, magazine, radio station or newspaper over another. In the end, consumers saw thousands of marketing messages every day, many of them irrelevant to them. While that model is still current, search is changing it. Search is allowing people to filter out the irrelevant messages and 'request' the relevant ones. This seems obvious in an online search environment like Google. It is also increasingly prevalent in other electronic media. Earlier, we discussed personal video recorders (PVRs). On the surface, a PVR is a digital recording device. Looked at through a different lens, a PVR is also a television search device, one that filters out programming and marketing messages that are irrelevant to the viewer.

Search, like all media, is also prone to convergence. For example, in 2008 YouTube, which is primarily a video entertainment site, surpassed Yahoo! as the source for the second-highest number of searches worldwide. Only Google was bigger. So, it is safe to ask, 'Is YouTube an entertainment site or a search engine?' Like so often in the online arena, the answer is 'both'.

> We believed we could build a better search. We had a simple idea, that not all pages are created equal. Some are more important.
>
> Sergey Brin
> Co-founder of Google

Potential futures of search

Search today is extremely effective, but let's face it, it is pretty dull. Impersonal computers and dogmatic mathematical algorithms spit back lines of text. From a visual perspective, about the most excitement you can count on is large font size and underlining. However, some advances in search are already starting to appear.

Search aided by a social interaction or a social connection is a paradigm shift in search, primarily because it does what everyone wants, it delivers 'human context' and therefore increased relevance. For example, when you ask a friend to recommend a restaurant, they consider your age, gender, ethnicity (demographics), where you live, what you both like in common, and because of your shared demographics they give you information only another human could give you... shared human contextual information. This type of search is what the Internet was created for... connecting people with like interests.

Robb Fujioka
Chairman
Fuhu Web Development

Video and audio are obvious places to look for greater degrees of 'engagingness' in search; Yahoo!, for example, has experimented with video results. But perhaps the most interesting potential future for search is *social search*. Imagine results that are ordered for you based on the recommendations of a vast extended social network of people like you. Depending on their relevance for the specific search, they may be like you in age, ethnicity, geographic location or attitudes. If you are looking for a good local restaurant, what might prove to be a more relevant source: an algorithm or people who live in your neighbourhood? A new search entrant from Sweden called 'Spezify' links both in a visual search that taps into social networks.

Personalised search is another interesting development. Caterina Fake, co-founder of Flickr, launched <Hunch.com>, which personalises results based on information that you give it about yourself.

Search will evolve to include many more features. It will become more engaging, entertaining and relevant. How quickly it evolves depends on how much competition there is in the search market. To date, due to Google's almost monolithic position, there has not been very much… but that might be changing soon. Next, we will look in-depth at a search engine from Microsoft, called 'Bing', which claims to have taken a step forward for improving the usefulness of search results.

⟨ From marketing push to consumer pull
Case study: Google versus Bing
⟩ Questions and exercises

Background

Google dominates search. In 2009, Google originated almost 70% of all search queries worldwide.[7] Google also owns YouTube which, as we have seen, can be considered the second largest search engine. Together, they dwarf number three: Yahoo!. In 2009, Yahoo!, once a high-flying online leader, responded to its position in the market place by agreeing to merge its search business with Microsoft.

Google is the number one site on the Web. It is number one in Turkey, Bulgaria, India, the United States and just about everywhere else, with the salient exception of China. And Google is still growing. Google is a company that is built to last, with a never-ending series of beta tests that allow it to grow and constantly evolve. As a result, Google is now more than a brand: it is a verb. To 'Google' something and to search for it are now synonymous. Google is the proverbial 800-pound gorilla in the search market. In 2009, it was named by the leading research company Millward Brown as the most valuable brand in the world for the third year running; its brand equity was calculated at $100 billion (£616 million).

Can Google be beaten?

Given the speed of digital change, Google will soon be beaten by new advances in search. The question is whether it will be beaten by itself or by someone else. For example, the fast-growing social networking site Friendster became so obsessed with growth and new products that it took its eye off the ball. The 'ball' was the quality and usability of their core product, the product that brought people to its site in the first place. Along came MySpace and now Friendster, to all intents and purposes, is history. Similarly, MySpace has quickly lost its leadership position to the more popular Facebook.

In order for Google to lose its footing, it is probably not enough for it to be distracted by growth. It will take a new search product that works better or delivers more relevant results. One might already exist. A major emerging competitor in the search space is Microsoft. In early 2009, Microsoft launched an innovative new product into the search market, which aims to be a serious challenger to Google's hegemony. It is called 'Bing'. Bing bills itself not as a search engine, but as a 'decision engine'.

Bing home page (right) and price predictor (below)

Bing's home page is designed to help searchers choose the best scope for their query. More unusually, the price predictor not only shows airfares, it also offers recommendations on whether to buy now or wait until later for a lower price. This added value has led to Microsoft calling Bing a 'decision engine'.

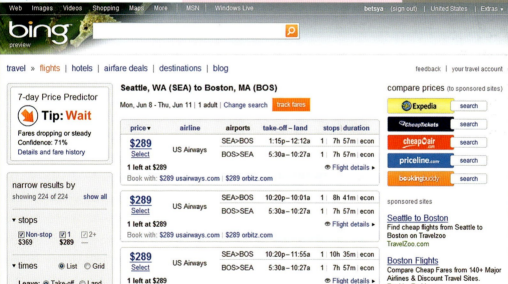

< From marketing push to consumer pull
Case study: Google versus Bing
> Questions and exercises

Bing

Bing aims to innovate search in two key ways. First, it wants to improve the ability to get the right information more quickly on simple searches. According to *BusinessWeek*: 'While Web surfers may say they are happy with search technology, the data shows that they don't find what they are after almost half the time....' So Microsoft developed a feature to avoid wasted effort: when users hover over a Web link without clicking, Microsoft's computers generate a pop-up summary of the link.

Secondly, Bing aims to improve consumers' ability to make complex decisions that involve more than a simple search. The site specialises in helping people to make decisions about travel, health, shopping and local area searches. As an example, the site has an airfare price predictor. It looks at price trends and historical information to suggest whether prices on your chosen route are likely to go up or down.

The future

So, will Bing carve out a significant market or even challenge Google for dominance? Microsoft is optimistic. One reason for their optimism is the recent merger between Bing and Yahoo! search. Another is the speed at which consumer usage of web software can shift. Think about how quickly the web browser Netscape went from being a dominant player with a runaway stock price to being dead. Look at how quickly its successor, Microsoft Explorer, was under siege from the likes of Safari, Firefox and Google Chrome. In search, think about how quickly AltaVista faded into the background and how quickly Yahoo! started showing cracks.

Conversely, some experts feel that Bing's innovations are good, but not revolutionary enough to hurt Google. Only time will tell. But greater competition in search will drive innovation and ultimately benefit consumers.

> The more I thought about it [challenging Google], the more it seemed like a duty.... There's a chance — a genuine chance — that we can make the search landscape a whole lot more competitive and healthy.
>
> Qi Lu
> Head of Microsoft Online Operations

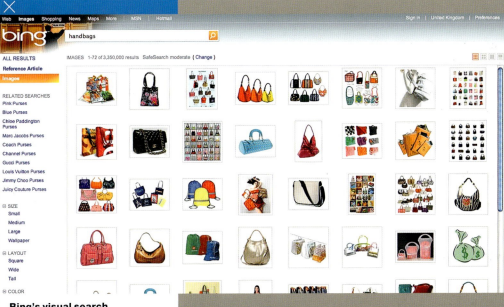

Bing's visual search

In September 2009, Bing announced a new feature called Visual Search, which allows users to easily find and filter information using images instead of text.

Question 1

What are Google's strengths and weaknesses? What are its opportunities and competitive threats?

Question 2

What other ways can you think of to make search results more useful, entertaining or relevant?

Question 3

Do you agree with Bing that there is a difference between a search engine and a decision engine. If so, why? If not, why not?

Questions and exercises

>

Discussion questions

1

Prior to reading this book, did you consider search as advertising? Why or why not?

2

If you had to put all of your search money into buying paid search ads or hiring people to create search optimisation strategies for your natural search, which would you do? Why?

3

What do you think search will look like in the future? Will Google continue to dominate? Ten years from now, how do you think you will input your search and what kind of results do you think you will get back?

Exercises

1

Search the keyword 'cosmetics'. What do the results tell you about the paid and natural search strategies of various competitors? In groups, develop a search optimisation strategy for one of the cosmetics companies that does not come up near the top.

2

Make a list of all the keywords and key phrases that the marketing director of Sony would want to buy in order to sell big-screen televisions. Which do you think would be more expensive? Which would be cheaper? With limited funds, would you buy expensive ones, cheap ones or a combination of both?

Summary

Search is the foundation of all online marketing. If consumers cannot find you, and find you quickly, you will be nearly invisible in the digital media marketplace. This is a dynamic field. You might be on top of the search engines one day and nowhere to be found the next. Continual search engine optimisation is key to continual success in natural search. Buying the right keywords or phrases at the right price is key to success in paid search.

Suggested further reading

Lieb, R. 2009. *The Truth About Search Engine Optimization: Searchers Either Find You, or They Find Your Competitors.* New Jersey: Pearson Education, Inc.

Verklin D. and Kanner B. 2007. *Watch This, Listen Up, Click Here: Inside the 300 Billion Dollar Business Behind the Media You Constantly Consume*, Chapter 14: Search: How Aubuchon Bested the Hardware Goliaths. New Jersey: John Wiley & Sons, Inc.

Endnotes

1
IAB Internet Advertising Report: 2009 full year results (April 2010). Retrieved from <www.iab.net> (10 April 2010)

2
Spiderhelp (2006). From Plummer, J., Rappaport, S. Hall, T, & Barocci, R. (2007). *The Online Advertising Playbook.* New Jersey: John Wiley & Sons, Inc.

3 and 4
Verklin, D. and Kanner, B. (2007). *Watch This, Listen Up, Click Here.* New Jersey: John Wiley & Sons, Inc.

5
Plummer, J., Rappaport, S., Hall, T. and Barocci, R. (2007). *The Online Advertising Playbook.* New Jersey: John Wiley & Sons, Inc.

6
Click Forensics and Anchor Intelligence. Retrieved from <http://blog.searchenginewatch.com> (10 April 2010)

7
Advertising Age: Digital Market Facts 2010

Find the things that make you look like you. Choose from an unparalleled selection of designer clothing, shoes, jewelry and accessories

This chapter looks at the Internet from two vital marketing perspectives: commerce and branding. We will look at what marketers need to do to successfully sell products online, as well as what it takes for them to build the image of their products online. We will specifically look at what attributes lead to strong brand websites. Some examples where marketers have got it wrong in the past are also provided.

A key aspect of online commerce and branding is the importance of collecting and analysing data. With this data, marketers are in a stronger position than ever before to measure the return on their marketing investment. We will look at how they monitor this, step-by-step, through the online purchase process, and compare it to how marketers did this historically using traditional methods. The chapter ends with a case study of eBay, a brand that has successfully mastered online commerce, built a strong online brand and much more.

**eBay –
pioneering e-commerce**
As this well-crafted advert from eBay makes clear, the Internet has opened up a dynamic channel for commerce – often offering consumers a much wider choice of products than they could find offline. In some cases, such as eBay, purchases are made directly. In others, commerce is facilitated by marketing websites. The ability to measure direct online sales, from e-commerce, and online actions that lead to sales, from e-branding, has vastly improved marketers' ability to measure return on investment (ROI).

The Internet as a storefront

Well before the Internet was seen as a medium with the marketing potential to build brands, it was envisioned as a storefront, a place to sell products with lower overheads, lower prices and higher profits. Many believed that the ease and cost of buying over the Internet would spell the end for bricks-and-mortar stores. In 1999 and 2000, dot.com storefronts on the Web boomed. By 2001, most of them went belly-up in the renowned 'dot.com bust'. Some weathered the storm because they had strong business models, and online shopping for the merchandise they offered added value for consumers. The best example is Amazon.

Amazon

Amazon started as an online bookstore. They guessed right that consumers would find it valuable to browse among millions of books online using a powerful search engine, and then be willing to wait a few days to receive discount books in the mail. In fact, when priority shipping is included, the books are often not discounted at all.

Such is the convenience of Amazon that it has been, and continues to be, a massive online success story. Since its launch it has expanded beyond books to other categories that consumers find easy to buy over the Web, such as music, toys, clothing, electronics and tools. Amazon also enhances the shopping experience by remembering its customers' preferences. They make recommendations about what their customers might want to buy next based on their previous purchases and those of people who bought the same or similar items. This gives Amazon a pseudo social network feeling.

As one of the first and most successful players in the dot.com space, Amazon also benefits from the fact that many people made their first Internet purchase with them. Long-term customers now trust Amazon with their credit card information and billing details. Since Amazon now sells a wide range of merchandise, many consumers use it as their single source for online shopping. This enables people to avoid giving their personal information to a variety of new websites.

greatest Debug Albums of all time
▶ Shop now at Amazon MP3

MP3 Daily Deal

Today's special: Jason Aldean's brand-new *Wide Open*, available exclusively at Amazon MP3 a day before you'll find it anywhere else. Everyday low price: $9.99
Today's price: **$3.99**

amazon MP3
Music Downloads for Any Device

Downloads instantly to:
🎵 iTunes Library
⊙ Windows Media Player

What's Happening at Amazon MP3

Browse MP3s

Most Popular

100 Greatest Indie Rock Albums of All Time

American Idol® Originals

ChordStrike Music Blog

Free Songs & Special Deals

MP3 Albums by Price

$4.99 and Under

$5.00 to $5.99

$6.00 to $6.99

$7.00 to $7.99

$8.00 to $8.99

Genres

Alternative & Indie Rock

Blues

Broadway & Vocalists

Children's Music

Christian & Gospel

Classic Rock

Classical: Instrumental

Classical: Opera & Vocal

Comedy & Miscellaneous

Country

Dance & Electronic

Folk

$7.99 Editors' Picks

Ray Guns Are Not Just the Future, the Bird and the Bee: $7.99

Blue Train, John Coltrane: $7.99

Quintana Roo, RH+: $7.99

› More $7.99 albums

$6.99 Bob Dylan Albums

Blonde on Blonde: $6.99

Highway 61 Revisited: $6.99

The Freewheelin' Bob Dylan: $6.99

› More by Bob Dylan

Free Music

"Mas Fuerte," CuCu Diamantes: $0.00

"Blanket" (Amazon MP3 Exclusive), Jeff Beck (feat. Imogen Heap): $0.00

"Pulling on a Line," Great Lake Swimmers: $0.00

› More free music

The 100 Greatest Indie Rock Albums

Bee Thousand, Guided by Voices: $9.99

In the Aeroplane Over the Sea, Neutral Milk Hotel: $9.99

Spiderland, Slint: $9.99

› See all 100 greatest indie rock albums

New and Notable MP3s

Page 1 of 4

Defying Gravity MP3 Download ~ Keith Urban
$8.99

R.O.O.T.S. [Explicit] MP3 Download ~ Flo Rida
$8.99

NOW 30 MP3 Download ~ Various Artists
$9.49

The Soundstage Sessions MP3 Download ~ Stevie Nicks
$8.99

Quiet Nights MP3 Download ~ Diana Krall
$8.99

Today's Top MP3 Songs

1. **Boom Boom Pow** by Black Eyed Peas
2. **Poker Face** by Lady GaGa
3. **Right Round** by Flo Rida

Today's Top MP3 Artists

1. **The Roots**
2. **Bat For Lashes**
3. **Keith Urban**

Amazon's MP3 store

Successful websites that started with specialist offerings have begun to diversify and expand their offerings. Amazon has now expanded beyond books to become a one-stop shop for everything from toys and MP3s to tools and gardening equipment.

<Pets.com>

Contrast the experience of Amazon with that of <pets.com>, which sold pet food, toys and accessories over the Web and was one of the early high-flyers of the dot.com boom. It is a cautionary tale about creating an online brand. It had extremely high brand awareness and a popular, high-profile advertising campaign. The campaign featured a charming animal sock puppet, which scored highly in audience recall in *USA Today*'s 'Ad Meter'. Yet, like many other dot.com businesses, <pets.com>'s lack of a strong business plan and its overly optimistic view of consumer demand for its products, led to its demise in less than one year. <Pets.com> spent $60 million (£40 million) in advertising and only generated $22 million (£15 million) in sales. Consumers did not find waiting a few days for dog food as convenient as waiting a few days for books. It's worth noting that the URL <pets.com> is now owned by PetSmart, Inc. who operate it as a 'Pet Parent' community.

The long tail

Online merchants take unique advantage of consumers who continue to buy products long after they initially become popular. The lack of physical space required for on-site inventory gives them a commercial leg-up on bricks-and-mortar stores. This ability to capture latent sales is known as 'the long tail'.

It is also worth noting that since the dot.com bust of the early 2000s, online retailing has again flourished, as consumers have become more comfortable buying things online.

In fact, one of the biggest shopping days of the year in the United States has been coined 'Cyber Monday'. It is the Monday after Thanksgiving when people are back at work and shopping online. In 2008 alone, $846 million (£57 million) was spent on this day, up 15% from 2007.[1] However, despite its growth, online sales still account for less than 5% of total retail sales in the US.[2]

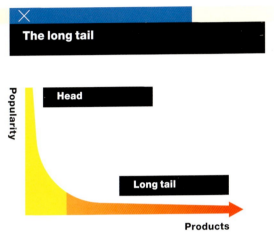

The long tail

Popularity

Head

Long tail

Products

The new marketplace

What brands such as Amazon exemplify is the value of having a vast inventory of items, many of which may sell in small numbers, versus specialisation or just stocking big sellers. Chris Anderson, editor-in-chief of *Wired* magazine, dubbed this the 'long tail'. The long tail is a description of the economic curve that reflects the people who continue to buy a product sporadically, long after it has become a 'hit' with a relatively short, high-volume burst of sales.

The Internet marketplace made long tail customers economically viable targets because it lowered the cost of making more products available to more people in more places.

In a physical store, where the product inventory is limited, it makes sense only to stock the hit items that will sell quickly and in large numbers. Internet-based companies like Amazon and online DVD rental stores, such as Netflix or LOVEFiLM, can 'have their cake and eat it' by selling large numbers of hit products, as well as steady levels of lower-selling products.

The long tail goes beyond books, music and movies. As David Verklin and Bernice Kanner note in *Watch This, Listen Up, Click Here*: '[the US-based airline] JetBlue, for example, has turned its website into a virtual department store, selling (in addition to plane tickets and model airplanes), jewellery, clothing, cosmetics, travel posters, office supplies, bar accessories and toys.'

The long tail means that, over time, airlines, bookstores, clothing stores and fast-food restaurants will be competing directly with each other to sell many of the same items to the same customers.

What happens when everything in the world becomes available to everyone? When the combined value of all the millions of items that may sell only a few copies equals or exceeds the value of the few items that sell millions each?

Chris Anderson
The Long Tail

< The Internet as a storefront
Online as a branding opportunity
> Building great brand websites

By the mid 2000s marketers started to embrace the Web as a medium for building brands and 'e-branding' was born. The first and most obvious branding opportunity was to transform websites from functional spaces intended only to provide brand information, or facilitate online purchasing, to multi-faceted brand experiences.

Brand websites today are deep, with many layers of content, and wide, with a broad range of segmented target audiences and subject areas. Therefore, they need to be built with three key goals in mind: *consistency*, *integration* and *flexibility*. A consistent website is one that provides the same level of quality and brand experience no matter which page of the website you land on. An integrated website is one that provides a brand experience that epitomises the messages and images created in all other media (traditional and digital). A flexible website is one that understands that the online space has special capabilities that make it a unique part of the media mix. Flexible websites take full advantage of those differences to enhance the consumer experience.

One of the best examples of a website that combines all three of these features is the US retailer Target. Wherever you land on the Target site, you are greeted by Target's distinctive bullseye logo and dominant red and white motif. It is entirely consistent in look and feel with the image created by its other advertising, such as its giant outdoor campaign in Times Square (shown opposite). It maintains flexibility by making full use of the functionality of the Web. The Target site is extremely deep and wide, and it offers incredible functionality, strong navigation, and interactive opportunities on almost every page.

E-branding pitfalls and pratfalls

There are many e-branding success stories, such as Target, but there are also many examples of brands that got it wrong, sometimes disastrously. The Web is a complicated place: it holds a vast amount of websites, each of which has mountains of information contained within it. It is by definition an interconnected place: a place where the people who interact with it have a lot of power. Marketers who get it wrong almost always underestimate either the complexity or the connectivity of the Web.

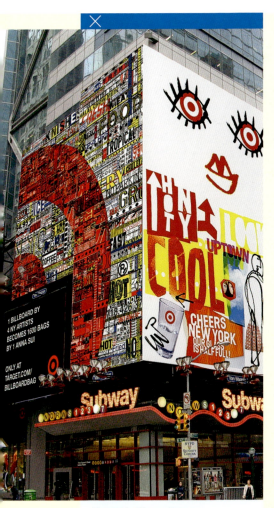

Target's Times Square outdoor advertisement
Target is a brand that brings powerful visual consistency to everything they do online and offline. Consistency between what a brand does on the Web and in its other media messages is important.

Mars Fling

To launch their new 85-calorie Fling chocolate bar, Mars embraced the idea of guiltless snacking with the campaign line '*Naughty, but not that Naughty*'. The website was targeted at women. It had a playful tone, taking full advantage of the naughty, flirtatious and alluring imagery conjured up by the product's name. It was replete with double entendres, but was never in bad taste. The website address was <www.flingchocolate.com>.

However, Mars underestimated the depth of the Web and the breadth of its content (both tasteful and sordid). They did not check to see that <www.fling.com>, which many people would understandably search for, was already taken by an adult personal services site, a site that specialised in connecting people who wanted to have a sexual fling. As a result, Mars was greeted by headlines such as the one in *Advertising Age* that said, 'Mars Sends Women Seeking New "Fling" to Porn Site'. One headline like that can erase months of hard work and can interfere with even the best product succeeding in the marketplace.

Building great brand websites

Great brand websites create engagement with their audience by meeting most or all of the following seven key criteria:

1
Branding
The site delivers on the brand's image and equity in the marketplace, as exemplified by its other advertising, both online and offline.

2
Completeness
The site takes advantage of the opportunities to provide depth and breadth of information and brand experience. As far as possible, it should provide everything a consumer could want to know about a brand, and as much as they could want to experience about it.

3
Functionality
One of the challenges of providing a complete site is to do so in a manner that makes it easy to navigate. Winning sites provide vast amounts of content that are logically organised and seemingly right at the consumer's fingertips.

4
Interactivity
In order for a site to be truly engaging it has to give the user a chance to get involved and offer input. The Web, by its nature, is an interactive medium. Sites that maximise interaction also maximise the length of time that consumers will stay on the site and experience the brand. Interactivity can include things as simple as being able to post ideas to a bulletin board or as immersive as online games.

5
Visual stimulation
The Web offers opportunities to use dynamic photography, Flash animation, and video instead of words and static photography alone. Cutting-edge websites maximise sight, sound and motion to entertain and inform their audiences.

6
Relevant advertising
Many websites include advertising. When this advertising is consistent with the site's subject or brand it can increase engagement, maximise relevance and improve functionality to users. When it is not, it increases annoyance and drives users away from the site.

7
Community connections
Great sites give their users the opportunity to connect with people like themselves to improve their online experience and enhance their relationship with the product or brand. For some products, like Procter & Gamble's Pampers, this is a natural step. They have created 'Pampers Village', offering what new parents most desire: an opportunity to share ideas with other new parents about raising children.

Stickiness

Sites that follow these seven principles are usually labelled as 'sticky'. **Stickiness** means that users stay on the site, or stick to it, for long periods of time. Sticky sites also tend to get people to come back to them again. Stickiness is a reflection of consumer engagement. In the traditional marketing model, brand messages put in front of consumers (such as advertising) are measured based on ratings, which measure how many people saw the message. Increasingly, brands are looking at a combination of how many people saw the message (on the Web this is called site traffic) and engagement. One example of this is a measurement called **brand engagement hours** (the total number of site visitors multiplied by time spent).

Navigation, word clouds and interactive elements

In the last chapter, we talked about the importance of keywords for successful search marketing. Keywords are also important for maximising the functionality of websites. Beyond the typical navigation bar, many sites offer a collection of words that link to specific, related content. These are often formatted as 'word clouds'. Words that relate to deep content appear larger, words that relate to thinner content appear smaller.

Another way to ensure high levels of engagement is to have the right amount, and the right mix, of interactive elements available to users. Mitch Winkels, a graduate student at Syracuse University, analysed the relationship between a site's ability to generate traffic and the number of interactive features it had made available. Features such as video games, avatars and social networking were considered.

He discovered that traffic increased when there were more interactive features on the site. However, he also found that when the number of interactive features was too high, users could become overwhelmed, which could actually decrease site traffic. There was also a premium on novelty: traffic increased when there were interactive features that were seen as cutting edge. The existence of social networking functions, for example, was directly correlated to traffic. Years ago, cutting edge might have been signalled by the existence of games on a site; today it is signalled by social networking.

✕

Running glossary

brand engagement hours
the number of people who visited the site multiplied by how long they stayed on it

stickiness
a site's ability to keep users engaged for long periods of time

Measuring return on investment (ROI)

> Case study: eBay develop e-commerce communities

The Web environment is digital, so it is easy to track and measure almost everything, such as site visits, length of time stayed, number of pages visited, inbound and outbound sites, requests for further information, actual purchase orders and so on. This new wealth of data has focused marketers on trying to precisely define the **return on investment (ROI)** of their marketing activities on the Web. ROI measures how much return, in money or actions that will lead to money, was generated versus the cost for building and maintaining the site and its cost-generating marketing components (such as promotions or offers).

The Web's ability to generate a constant stream of data to help calculate ROI is making it increasingly popular with marketers. This is because they have long suffered from the inability of traditional media advertising to provide measures beyond the total number of people they reached and the number of times they reached them. Therefore, online marketing has a decided advantage in ROI measurement over traditional advertising. Online marketing is perceived by marketing directors and top management to be more accountable.

One-step and two-step marketing processes

When the goal of a website is to generate an immediate sale, ROI calculation is relatively straightforward because the cost of the sale, or the profit from it, can define the 'return'. This is known as a 'one-step marketing process'. But what about cases where the site is supposed to cultivate customers for an eventual sale at a later date? The goal of many sites is to get people to see information or request information that may have a specific relationship to an eventual sale. For example, marketers in different industries know that a certain proven percentage of people who request a brochure for their product will go on to buy it. This is called a 'two-step marketing process'. ROI measurement in a two-step online process is not necessarily straightforward.

Regardless of whether a site is intended to be a one-step or two-step process, the Web gives marketers an unparalleled ability to estimate ROI. A key to making this calculation is to define something called **conversion**.

Running glossary

conversion

the percentage of unique visitors who take a desired action online that will directly or eventually produce revenue

return on investment (ROI)

a performance measure for evaluating the efficiency of an investment. ROI is calculated by dividing the benefit (return) by the cost of the investment; the result is expressed as a percentage or a ratio

Conversion

Conversion is simply the percentage of 'unique' visitors to your site who take a desired action that either directly or indirectly produces revenue. Online marketers use the term 'unique visitors' to define individual visitors as opposed to the total number of visits or hits, since some people visit more than once. It is roughly equivalent to the term 'reach' in traditional marketing.

When a site's goal is to generate an immediate sale, as is the case with <Amazon.com> for example, conversion is equal to the percentage of people who buy something. Sales drive revenue directly. On other sites, conversion can be something that leads indirectly to an eventual sale, such as requesting more information, viewing a key section or page, providing sales leads, or downloading something specific, such as a white paper. Importantly, conversion is always concrete and measurable.

Half the money I spend on advertising is wasted; the trouble is I don't know which half.

John Wanamaker
Merchant and politician
(1838–1922)

< Building great brand websites
Measuring return on investment (ROI)
> Case study: eBay develop e-commerce communities

A new consumer purchase funnel

The centrality of conversion in online marketing is changing the way in which marketers view consumer purchasing habits. For decades, the cornerstone of marketing theory as it relates to consumer purchasing has been the 'purchase funnel'. The purchase funnel, as defined by marketing consulting companies such as Alison-Fisher International, describes the cognitive processes that consumers go through when making a purchase decision (particularly for more expensive items, such as cars, refrigerators, expensive clothing and so on).

Consumers begin the process by becoming *aware* of the product or brand. Then they may *consider* it as an alternative to other brands. They may start to *prefer* it to other brands. Then they may purchase it. If they purchase, they decide whether to *re-purchase* it or not. Marketers attempt to influence the consumer in specific stages of the funnel by targeting specific messages to specific audiences at specific stages of the purchase consideration process. In other words, some messages are intended to drive general awareness and/or consideration of the brand at the top of the funnel (for example, brand advertising); while other messages are intended to drive competitive preference and/or purchase (for example, a sales promotion) at the bottom of the funnel.

Online purchase model

The emergence of online marketing – and the newfound importance of conversion as a measurable goal – has led to the development of an 'online purchase funnel' (see page 64). The online purchase funnel does not negate the traditional purchase funnel, which is about *cognition*. It augments it as a new tool, which is about online *actions* and *behaviour*.

While the traditional purchase funnel is about delivering the right message at the right time, the online purchase funnel is focused on measuring the right data and continually improving numerical results. The online funnel is used to help marketers to maximise conversion and return on investment (ROI). There is an old saying, 'You can't manage what you can't measure.' The online funnel is all about measurement. The traditional funnel and the online funnel are best used together: they complement each other. They help marketers to get the right message out at the right time and to measure the right consumer actions at the right stage.

The online funnel looks first at the number of visits/hits, and click-throughs on the site. It measures the number of unique visitors who generated those hits and click-throughs. It narrows them down to qualified unique visitors (in other words, the number who fit a profile that indicates that they are likely to purchase the product). It then tracks the specific conversion percentage. The goal of the top half of the funnel is to maximise the numbers and percentages in each box in order to maximise conversion and/or purchase.

The traditional purchase funnel
The traditional purchase funnel
describes the cognitive processes
that consumers go through over
the time between when they first
hear about a brand and when they
first buy it.

>

The traditional purchase funnel

Awareness

Consideration

Preference

Purchase

Retention

Once conversion has been measured
and maximised, the value of the eventual
transactions are calculated. The online
funnel looks not only at the total current
value of those transactions (the total number
of transactions multiplied by the average
monetary value per transaction), but also at
the lifetime value of the transactions. This is
critical, because online marketing is about
creating a relationship. Relationships are
long-term affairs. Once someone has been
induced to buy your product, every time he or
she continues to buy it the relative cost of
marketing goes down and the ROI goes up
sharply. Therefore, leading-edge brands
measure both short-term and long-term ROI.

< Building great brand websites
Measuring return on investment (ROI)
> Case study: eBay develop e-commerce communities

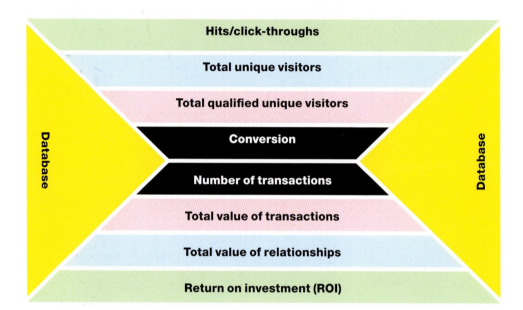

The online purchase funnel

The online purchase funnel supplements the traditional purchase funnel by measuring online behaviour and tracking the steps that lead to conversion and ROI measurement.

Data, data and more data

E-commerce and e-branding are often referred to as being 'data-driven'. This is because the online marketing process generates data at every step, and successful management of the process entails making the most out of this information. However, because every consumer visit and action online generates data, it can be easy for marketers to become overwhelmed by a sea of information.

The first step in dealing with data is to define what data is useful for driving your key revenue engine (i.e. conversion) and what data is useful for maximising ROI. In other words, you need to segment 'good data' – the data that drives your business – from 'bad' data – the information that leads nowhere.

An important point about data is that even bad data can be very useful. Your bad data can be someone else's good data. You can share it with other brands in your company or sell it to other companies. (Note: brands do best when they gain permission from consumers before they share or sell any kind of data to others.)

Where the data guys were once an afterthought in a marketing presentation, now they are at the core of the online strategy.

New York Times
30 May 2009

A potential example here is the clothing company Gap Inc., which owns a variety of clothing brands that target different audiences, such as Gap, Old Navy and Banana Republic. People who visit certain parts of the Gap website, for example, and do not buy or reach conversion, might be excellent candidates to buy or convert for Banana Republic instead. In this case, choosing to share data between divisions could be very helpful. Similarly, sharing between companies sometimes makes sense. People who used an automotive site to configure a new car, for example, could be excellent leads for an insurance company.

We will cover data analysis in further detail in Chapter 7.

Background

A chapter including e-commerce would not be complete without mentioning one of the Web's most dominant commercial brands: eBay. eBay is more than an online market; it is an online marketplace. A *market* is a place that people visit in order to buy something. A *marketplace* is where both buyers and sellers go to show their wares and negotiate sales with each other.

Like Amazon, eBay is one of the survivors of the dot.com boom of the late 1990s. Similar to many online success stories, it had modest beginnings, with founder Pierre Omidyar selling a broken laser pointer via the Internet for $13.83 in 1995. Since then, it has survived and thrived because it was one of the first players in its domain, and it is unquestionably the best and most trusted at what it does.

In a similar way to Google's position in search, eBay has become an almost generic term for buying and selling over the Web. As an online marketplace (and as one of the first big, successful websites), eBay was fundamental in shaping the development of the Web. By transforming its e-commerce site into an e-commerce community, it became one of the first sites for consumers to congregate with each other, as opposed to relating to the site itself. eBay doesn't sell anything; eBay is a social enabler. It facilitates people dealing with other people, for a profit. As we will discuss in further detail in Chapter 5, communities and social networks are the most important recent development on the Web from a marketing perspective.

If eBay employed the... people who earn an income selling on its site, it would be the [United State's] No. 2 private employer, behind Wal-Mart.

David Faber
Business, finance/tax, journalism speaker

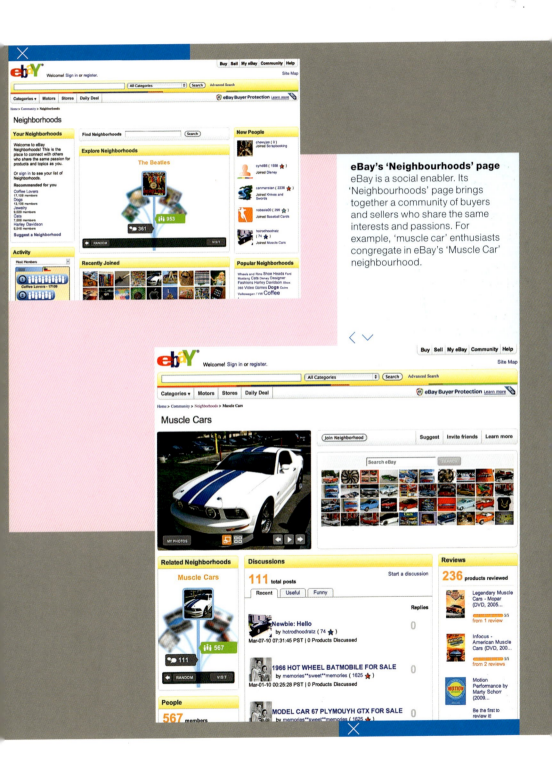

eBay's 'Neighbourhoods' page

eBay is a social enabler. Its 'Neighbourhoods' page brings together a community of buyers and sellers who share the same interests and passions. For example, 'muscle car' enthusiasts congregate in eBay's 'Muscle Car' neighbourhood.

‹ Measuring return on investment (ROI)
Case study: eBay develop e-commerce communities
› Questions and exercises

An online community

Much more than just giving their customers a place to congregate, eBay have been at the forefront of providing the tools that people need to maximise their involvement in online communities (such as discussion boards, groups, blogs and chat rooms). They even have a feature called 'eBay Neighbourhoods', which allows people to connect to other people who share their passions, such as baseball, horse riding, or French handbags, and to do business with them on related merchandise. In many ways, eBay can be considered the Web's first social networking site.

The power, reach and scale of eBay's social networks are vast. It has a staggering 81 million unique visitors per month. It competes on a local community level with flea markets. It even competes on a global basis with high-priced brokers like Christie's and Sotheby's. For example, a rare music collection including six million songs on three million records and 300,000 compact discs sold on eBay for $3 million (£2 million)! Its reach has created a broad global trading market that simultaneously drives down prices and maximises the value that can be garnered for any unique item. In 2009, a 1985 collectable Christmas Bear from British retailer Harrods, which originally sold for £14.95, sold on eBay for £500 ($750).

A short economics lesson

eBay is a prime example of how the Web is creating new markets for trade and is unlocking the economic efficiencies of the global marketplace. eBay is an economist's dream. It allows ease of goods transfer on a global basis, and brings together millions of individuals to bid on specific products in a way that gives them maximum satisfaction (economists call this 'utility') from selling and buying items at perceived fair-market value. eBay has created a market that gets close to optimal efficiency (economists call this 'pareto optimal'), defined as improving the satisfaction of both buyer and seller to a point where almost no further improvements can be made.

Question 1

Look at the eBay site. Are there any new features they could provide to enhance buying and selling? Are there any that would foster a tighter community?

Question 2

Which do you think would be better value: a used tennis racket purchased at a local flea market or one purchased over eBay? Why?

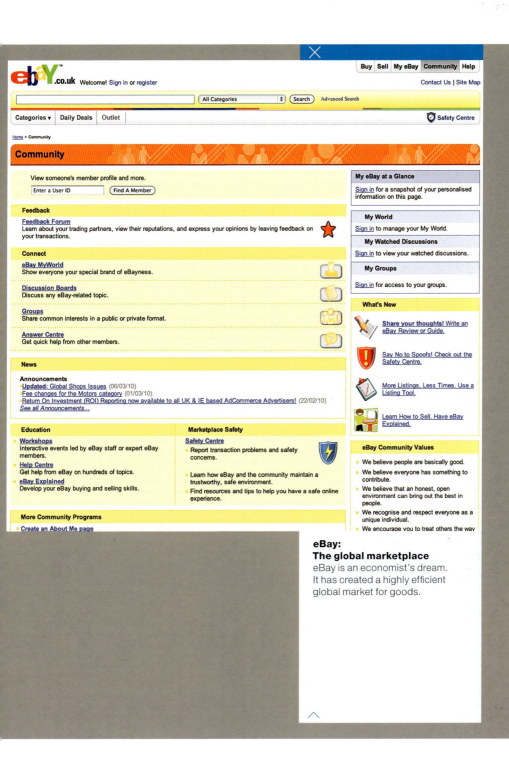

eBay:
The global marketplace
eBay is an economist's dream.
It has created a highly efficient
global market for goods.

Questions and exercises

⟩

Discussion questions

1

What websites do you feel confident purchasing from? Why do you use those sites and not others?

2

Measuring online return on investment (ROI) has become somewhat of an obsession in marketing today. Are there any potential downsides to this emphasis on measuring ROI? Hint: there are!

3

Why might a brand prefer a two-step process to a one-step process when designing their website? Similarly, why would you look at anything but sales as your measure of conversion online?

Exercises

1

Spend 15 minutes surfing the websites of the first five or six brands you can think of. Which ones best meet the criteria for 'building great brand websites' shown on page 58?

2

Make a list of products that are particularly advantaged by being able to cash in on 'long tail' sales over the Internet.

3

Copy a few paragraphs of text that you have written or text from any other digital source and enter it into <www.wordle.com> to create your own word cloud. Compare the word cloud (both the words and the relative sizes of the words) to the original text.

4

Consider a company like L'Oréal. Develop a brief strategy for how they might share online data between each of their brands to improve their success in the top of the online purchase funnel, and ultimately their conversion.

Summary

E-commerce and e-branding are marketing goals that can be accomplished with successful websites. Great websites are 'sticky'; they make people want to visit the site, stay on it for an extended period and come back again, often. They create stickiness by enhancing consumer engagement. Some things that lead to strong consumer engagement are easy functionality, interactive features, visual stimulation, relevant advertising and community connections.

Suggested further reading

Anderson, C. 2008. *The Long Tail: Why the Future of Business is Selling Less of More.* New York: Hyperion

McFadyen, T. 2008. *Ecommerce Best Practices: How to Market, Sell, and Service Customers with Internet Technologies.* Virginia: McFadyen Solutions

Endnotes

1
Kafka, P. (3 December 2008). ComScore: Cyber Monday sales up 15%. 'The Wall Street Journal Digital Network'. Retrieved from <http://mediamemo.allthingsd.com/20081203/comscore-cyber-monday-sales-up-15/> (30 May 2009)

2
U.S. Census Bureau. Retrieved from <www.marketingcharts.com> (10 April 2010)

Find your passion.

Yahoo! Careers

Do you believe in destiny?

How's that working out?

Maybe it's time to believe in Yahoo! Careers.

Check out tons of job listings. Post your resume.

Give destiny a little boost.

careers.yahoo.com

DO YOU YAHOO!?

By 2011, online advertising is projected to account for 15.6% of all advertising spending.[1] By 2014, it is projected to account for 21%. This chapter looks at online advertising techniques. After looking at basic display ads, we will explore more creative uses of advertising on the Web, ideas that take full advantage of the medium's connectivity and interaction. We will look at a number of examples, including one of the earliest and best: BMW Films. Another key advertising approach online is e-mail marketing. We will explore how e-mail marketing is a double-edged sword where it is very easy to get it wrong by annoying potential customers.

New online approaches to advertising are also mounting a challenge to the age-old process by which advertising agencies develop creative campaigns and plan media. We will highlight the emerging importance of *context* for both creative and media development. The chapter ends with a case study of one of the Web's most successful and creative advertisers: Burger King.

Offline advertising for online products

As this eye-catching magazine advert for Yahoo! demonstrates, sometimes the best way to generate traffic for an online product is to advertise it offline. This is because the Web is typified by its diversity and fragmentation, meaning that print and television adverts are often the best way to reach a very broad audience.

<

The Internet poses a significant challenge to traditional advertising and the process that advertising agencies go through in planning, creating and executing advertising. *Advertising Age* columnist Bob Garfield has gone so far as to compare the entrenched advertising establishment to the planet Pluto, which was ensconced in the firmament of our solar system only to be downgraded a few years ago to 'dwarf planet' status.

Pluto is no longer considered good enough to be a planet any more. Like Pluto, old traditional advertising methods are being downgraded in their perceived importance in the advertising mix. Marketing and advertising professionals are being challenged as never before to quickly create advertising strategies and tactics more in tune with the immense capabilities of digital media.

Display ads are one of the first places marketers look when they are developing online advertising strategies.

Display ads

When you think of advertising on the Web, you most likely think of display advertising. Display ads are the ads you often notice first when you visit websites. Like small space newspaper ads, they take up a certain set space on the web page. They are defined as Interactive Marketing Units (IMUs) and are measured in pixels. Some of the most common sizes and shapes are:

Banner ads

Banners are the most common type of ad running horizontally on the page. When they run across the full top of the web page, they are called 'leaderboards'. A typical banner ad is 468 × 60 pixels.

Skyscrapers

Skyscrapers are tall vertical ads that run along the side of the page, usually the right-hand side. A typical skyscraper is 160 × 600 pixels.

Rectangles

Rectangles are exactly that, although to the naked eye they look like a square box. A large rectangle is 336 × 280 pixels.

Buttons

Buttons look like small rectangle ads. A typical button is 120 × 90 pixels.

Display ads come in many size and shape variations of the basic units listed above.

Der Spiegel website with display advertisements

This page on the website for the German magazine *Der Spiegel* shows standard-sized rectangle and skyscraper display ads side by side.

Getting the most from display ads

Regardless of size, it pays to follow some specific guidelines when trying to get the most out of your display ads. <webtips.com> offers seven practical tips, from marketing executive Michael Fleischner, for increasing the click-through for online display ads:

■ Design your ad for specific sites
■ Animate your ad
■ Keep copy brief and provocative
■ Test multiple design formats
■ Use a professional graphics artist
■ Reduce the file size of your ad to improve loading speed
■ Evaluate performance daily

Now, say hello to Pluto — the suddenly former planet. Forever and immutable, it turns out, are subject to demotion. This could be grim news for the agency business, which continues its erratic Pluto-like orbit around marketing budgets as if unaware that it has lost its stature — and its relevance is next to go. In due course, you shall see how circumstances have conspired to threaten its place on the cosmic map altogether.

Bob Garfield
Advertising Age

Interactivity

Display ads involve various levels of interactivity. Some are static. Some have animation. Some have video. Some expand. Some interact with other display ads on the page. Some transform or move when rolled over by the cursor.

Despite their ubiquity, display ads have very low levels of engagement and click-through. Google estimates that display ads have a click-through rate of only 0.1%.[2] They are extremely easy to ignore. When advertisers make them too intrusive, by making them pop up or having them come up before you get to your website (known as 'interstitial' ads), they can become annoying to the user and can hinder the advertiser as much as they help.

In order to improve the performance of display ads, the Online Publishers Association (OPA) recently introduced three new, larger units – since larger units have slightly higher engagement and click-through rates. The new units are:

The fixed panel

As wide as a large rectangle and much taller. This is 336 × 860 pixels.

The XXL box

A similar large box that opens for seven seconds to double its width, dominating the page. This is 468 × 648 pixels.

The pushdown

A large box, which opens to display the ad and then rolls up to a banner-type ad after seven seconds. This is 970 × 418 pixels.

These new ad formats have been coined 'supersized' display ads. The hope is that the larger size will lead to better results and drive more advertising money to websites.

Of course, like traditional advertising, display ads have value even when people do not click on them. While they might not drive conversion and sales in the online purchase funnel, they do increase awareness and affect preference cognitively as described in the traditional purchase funnel. A recent study by ComScore, looking at people exposed to display ads for the 80 biggest campaigns across 200 high-traffic sites, found that:

- 20% conducted related search queries
- More than 30% visited the brand's site
- They spent 50% more time on the site
- They spent 10% more money [3]

Cost per thousand (CPM)

In Chapter 2, when we looked at search advertising, we noted that search ads were priced on a cost-per-click (CPC) basis. Display ads are priced on either a CPC or a 'cost-per-thousand' (CPM) basis. In general, ads on websites that generate a lot of traffic or clicks tend to work on a CPC basis. Ads on websites that cannot count on generating a lot of traffic or clicks sometimes use the CPM method as a way of garnering a minimum revenue/cost for the space. CPM sets a price based on the cost of every thousand people who see the ad, as opposed to the number who click on it. This is similar to the way in which television media is priced.

A little more history: Meet John Caples

In some ways, perhaps, writing for the Web is not entirely different from writing traditional ads. Specifically, they are similar to writing small space print ads, which compete directly with the editorial in newspapers and magazines. In his landmark book, *Tested Advertising Methods*, first published in 1932, John Caples gave the following advice to copywriters writing small space ads:

'Use telegraphic language…. The sentence, "We will be glad to mail you a copy of our free booklet on request," can be condensed to two words, "Free Booklet"…. One way to produce a good small ad is to take a big ad and boil down the copy. Cut out the introduction. Cut out the sentences with the least selling power. Omit all unnecessary words. Use short words in place of long words…. By the time a page ad is cut down to a half-column there is not an ounce of fat left in the ad. It is bone and muscle, and it frequently pulls several times its weight in sales.'

Writing display ads for the Web

One of the keys to writing effective online display ads is to keep copy short and provocative. To be effective, online ads need to attract the interest of users who are browsing or surfing for specific information and ignoring the rest. Using a combination of words, graphics and motion, the ad needs to break through to the viewer and elicit a response.

The words are particularly important because they are usually the thing that gets people to act, click or convert once the ad is noticed. In their book *Advertising Principles and Practice*, William Wells, Sandra Moriarty and Nancy Mitchell suggest that copywriters for Web ads bear the following thoughts in mind in order to make their ads more effective:

- Offer a deal that promises a discount or a freebie as a prize.

- Use an involvement device such as a challenge or contest.

- Change the offer frequently, perhaps even daily. Good ads exploit the 'nowness' and 'newsiness' of the Web.

- Keep the writing succinct, because most surfers have short attention spans on the Web and get bored easily.

- Focus surfers' attention by asking provocative questions or offering knowledge that they can use.

- Use the advertisement to solicit information and opinions from users and offer them fun or captivating rewards for sharing that information.

‹ Display advertising
Advertising creativity beyond display ads
› E-mail marketing

Display ads are the most basic form of online advertising. In many ways they are remnants of the early days of the Web, when advertisers treated a web page as the equivalent of an online magazine or newspaper page. More recently, advertisers have explored more creative and interactive online advertising approaches. Here we will look at some of the most promising, including video ads, branded content and viral ads.

The most significant recent development in online advertising has been the explosion of video advertising. If the early days of the Web were more like print advertising, the current state of the Web is looking a lot more like TV. Unlike TV, which in most countries uses a standard unit (for example, the 30-second spot or advert), online video ads can appear in a wide variety of lengths. They are usually categorised as 'short form' (adverts that are less than two minutes long) or 'long form' (ads that are two minutes or longer). They are also segmented into ads that take the form of ads (and that are clearly trying to sell you something) and ads that provide sponsored or 'branded' content (such as information or entertainment).

One of the most popular video ad placements is the 'pre-roll' ad. This is a short ad – usually 15 seconds in length – that precedes the viewing of some video content on a website, like a video recap of the Wimbledon tennis final on a sports site for example. These ads interrupt the viewing process, just as traditional TV ads do. However, 15 seconds seems to be a length of interruption that most people will accept in order to see the quality video that follows.

Running glossary

viral marketing
online marketing messages that are so funny or interesting that people share them electronically with friends, family and acquaintances

Long-form branded content

Longer video ads of two minutes or more are often placed within display ads, video windows on web pages, or on a product's home website. They try to entice the consumer to click on them in order to enjoy the product information or entertainment that they provide. Sometimes these longer ads look like ads; sometimes they are indistinguishable from content.

BMW was a trailblazer in long-form branded content. In 2001 and 2002, BMW produced and aired eight short films on the Web under the banner *The Hire*. The films were shot by A-list directors such as Ang Lee, John Frankenheimer and Guy Ritchie. All eight films were very different, but they consistently featured a few key things: action, BMW automobiles and the actor Clive Owen as the driver. The films were mini movies of eight to ten minutes each. In one film, called *The Ambush*, Owen drives an elderly gentleman who is supposedly carrying a fortune in diamonds. They are ambushed by a van full of armed men, and a full-scale Hollywood-style chase ensues. The bullet-ridden BMW survives, as do Owen and his passenger.

BMW was years ahead of its time. It has inspired many brands to take advantage of the unique characteristics of the Web to entertain and inform online audiences with their advertising and products, instead of just showing them TV ads online. Similarly, Ritz-Carlton hotels offered up a series of ten-minute films that take place in and around their hotels in an effort to engage a younger audience and to refresh their image.

Viral marketing

The success of BMW's films success also had a lot to do with buzz, and people sharing the films with others (in the first four months, 94% of the site's registrants recommended the films to others). This was an early indication of the power of communities on the Web to make content and advertising succeed virally. Today, marketers see tremendous potential in **viral marketing**. It is extremely attractive. The content might cost money to produce, but the media cost is extremely low if people are sending it to other people for you. Unfortunately, just wanting to have something 'go viral' and actually being able to do it are two very different things. In fact, only a tiny percentage of online ads or branded content that is produced to be viral actually succeeds.

A few things that successful viral ads tend to have in common are:

■ They avoid hard product sell. The branding and use of the product is either subtle or completely natural and relevant.

■ They elicit strong emotions. They are extremely funny, extremely interesting or extremely riveting. The emphasis is on 'extremely'. Good is not good enough.

■ They make you want to share them. People will thank you for passing them on, not see them as annoying junk mail.

〈 Display advertising
Advertising creativity beyond display ads
〉 E-mail marketing

Quiksilver

A great example of viral success comes from Denmark. Quiksilver, the surfing brand, shot an amazing 82-second film on Copenhagen's Lake Sortedams. It comes across as a guerrilla video, shot on a handheld camera. It features a group of hooded teenagers, one of whom wades his surfboard out into the middle of the lake while another throws a sizzling stick of dynamite into the lake. After a tremendous explosion, a big wave forms, which the surfer rides expertly.

The Quiksilver video was an instant smash hit. People all over the world sent the link to friends and over ten million people have viewed it on YouTube. The film ends with a simple Quiksilver logo. Because the brand fits so naturally in the story, and we never see one of those overt product close-ups in the film, the Quiksilver logo feels natural. The brand is given credit by the consumer, and praised for engaging the emotions and providing a piece of film that people want to share with their friends. It proves that Quiksilver is cool. They don't just say they are cool, they know how to create online advertising in a cool and confident way.

Quiksilver Dynamite Surfing
Authenticity can be the key to increasing the 'spreadability' of viral films. Quiksilver's *Dynamite Surfing* video shows that brands can create viral videos that feel authentic, while being strongly branded at the same time.

Original thinking

< Display advertising
Advertising creativity beyond display ads
> E-mail marketing

Entertainment value

Another terrific viral marketer is Cadbury, the British chocolate company. In support of their branding idea that each Cadbury bar tastes better because it contains a 'glass and a half' of real milk, they have created a number of films under the banner of 'Glass and a Half Full Productions'. Each video is offbeat, fun and begs to be shared with friends. In one we see a close-up of a gorilla, set to Phil Collins' eerie, macabre soundtrack *In the Air Tonight*. We pull back just in time to see the gorilla expertly pound the drums in the song's defining drum solo.

In another Cadbury online video, we see two children sitting for a portrait who start moving their eyebrows in sync with the digital pop music coming from the boy's watch. They are pure nonsense, but they are fun nonsense that you want to send to friends immediately. They end with the line: 'A Glass and a Half Full of Joy'. They are a joy, and viral gold.

Similarly, Procter & Gamble (P&G) recently launched an unusual and very subtly branded series of viral films about a teenage boy who wakes up with 'girl parts' for their Tampax brand.

Some viral videos work and others do not. The key is to constantly experiment. As a P&G spokesman put it, they were just 'playing around with some different ideas', adding that it was inexpensive and they were testing the waters to see if people would pick it up and share it.[4]

Online advertising has sparked a revolution in creativity, in part because it has opened up so many options in terms of ad length and position. Is there an optimal length for video ads? There is not enough research to know yet. One study, by Internet advertising firm Lotame, pegs it at about 40 seconds. According to their study, 'a measurable increase in a person's intent to view begins after 17 seconds of exposure to an ad, peaks at 76 seconds, and significantly degrades after 225 seconds.'[5] In another interesting development, 88% of people who watch TV programming on <Hulu.com> prefer to see one two-minute ad rather than four 30-second ads.[6]

Asking which length is optimal seems to miss the point, however, and threatens to restrict us to standardised options, like the 30-second TV ad. The Web proves every day that a variety of adverts of different lengths can work. If your ad is a straight sales pitch, better to keep it short. If it is extremely interesting, funny or riveting, it can be as long as it needs to be, for as long as it stays that way.

Cadbury's viral advertisement
Most people share videos with friends and family because they are entertaining. Cadbury's 'Gorilla' video is pure entertainment, with a branded message, that just begs to be shared with others.

Another web-based communication option is e-mail. E-mail campaigns can be very cost effective because they are so cheap to produce. According to a Forrester research study, a direct mail campaign to a company's in-house list costs $761/£480 per thousand mail-outs. An e-mail campaign to the same list costs $5/£3 per thousand.[7] However, consumers have a low tolerance for e-mail messages that they consider junk, or spam. It is a bit of a conundrum for marketers because, as Shelly Rogers of the University of Missouri and Qimei Chen of University of Hawaii discovered in their research, the people who are most motivated to use e-mail are also the ones most likely to find spam an intrusion.[8]

Opt-in and opt-out

The best way to resolve this is to develop e-mail campaigns that request the permission of the consumer to continue. This is done in one of two ways, called **opt-in** and **opt-out**. Opt-in campaigns are where the consumer requests to continue receiving the e-mailings. For example, the consumer would select a box saying that they want to receive future offers, online newsletters and so on by e-mail. If the consumer does not opt-in then they will receive nothing more. Opt-out is where the consumer will continue to receive the e-mails unless they select the box or e-mail back that they would like to stop receiving the e-mails, and to be taken off the mailing list.

Opt-in campaigns give the consumer more control, but either approach respects the consumer by asking for their permission to continue sending them e-mail. Once the consumer has granted permission, there is little chance that they will see future e-mails as spam. The biggest mistake that a marketer can make in e-mail marketing is to continue to send e-mails that the consumer does not want.

For the launch of the PlayStation 2 in Australia, Sony cleverly combined a website, e-mail with a creative opt-out option, and viral marketing to generate campaign success. On the website consumers were invited to fill out a form to enter a prize draw. If they gave the e-mail address of a friend they would receive another entry to win the prize.

Rather than use a traditional 'No' box to opt-out, they offered the cheeky option, 'Sorry, I don't have any friends.' As a thank you, they got a free downloadable screen saver that they could also share with friends virally.

The e-mail blast component was incredibly successful, with 30% of e-mail recipients entering the contest. When you consider that direct mail would have been hugely successful at a 5% or 6%, response, and would have cost a lot more to produce, e-mail was a big winner for Sony. Sony also supplemented the names they garnered from the opt-out mechanism with an opt-in database of 50,000 additional gamers.[9]

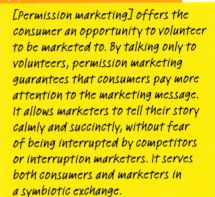

[Permission marketing] offers the consumer an opportunity to volunteer to be marketed to. By talking only to volunteers, permission marketing guarantees that consumers pay more attention to the marketing message. It allows marketers to tell their story calmly and succinctly, without fear of being interrupted by competitors or interruption marketers. It serves both consumers and marketers in a symbiotic exchange.

Seth Godin
Author of *Permission Marketing*

Running glossary

opt-in
this gives the consumer an opportunity to request to receive e-mails from a specific marketer

opt-out
this gives the consumer the opportunity to request to stop receiving e-mails from a specific marketer

< E-mail marketing
New approaches to creative media
> When is offline the best way to advertise online?

In the traditional advertising model, the connection between planning the media and developing the creative executions was often tenuous. The media planners would usually plan and buy the space months before the creative teams would start developing the work to fill that space. Often, the media planners, the creative copywriters and art directors never actually met to discuss how they could maximise the connection between *what* was running and *where* it was running. One reason for this was that media lengths and positions were pretty cut and dried: 30-second commercials, full-page newspaper ads and so on. Also, it was far too expensive to create separate executions for separate shows or magazines. Therefore, one execution ran across many different types of programming.

Contextual planning and the creative brief

The Internet has changed all that. Now, in a fragmented media space where modifying creative executions is relatively inexpensive, there is a premium on matching content to programming. This has led to a new planning approach, which brings media planners and creative developers closer together, called *contextual planning*. The emphasis is on the context within which the message will appear. When content matches context, the relevance to the consumer is enhanced. As we learned in Chapter 2, most experiences on the Web start with consumer intent, so when an expectant mother goes to a website for mothering tips, a Pampers ad in that context is highly relevant.

Contextual relevance goes far beyond matching sites to content; it includes matching messages to a consumer's mindset in different contexts. For example, if a consumer is visiting a comedy website, a humorous ad would make sense. This can drill down to very specific content. If a consumer is reading about an accident on a news site, it might be the right context for a car insurance ad.

Increasingly, advertising agencies are dealing with the need to marry content and context by combining the processes by which they brief their creative and media employees.

They do this by using a 'contextual creative brief', which is given to both teams simultaneously, and which is developed with the input of both the top media people and top creative people in the organisation.

Aside from matching content to context, digital media has opened up a plethora of new options for planning media placements. Because Internet-based operations are easily tracked, it is now simpler than ever to target specific groups of consumers based on criteria such as online behaviour and geography.

Geographical targeting allows advertisers to serve up focused online messages to people in specific parts of the world and even different regions within particular countries. This is obviously useful for regional brands, but it is also useful for brands that have different pricing, promotions or product options for different geographic locations, or brands that want to test a new product in a certain area. Unlike TV, for example, online geographic isolation can be cut very thin. For example, a price message or feature in an ad for a laptop can be different for people who live close to the retailer in one part of a city than for those people who live further away in another part of the same city.

Behavioural targeting

Behavioural targeting is even more dynamic. Different messages can be served up to consumers based on their pattern of online behaviour. In other words, if a consumer has come to your site through a series of other sites or navigated your site in a particular way, or if they have a history of visiting certain sites, you can match your message to their online behaviour. For example, if someone goes to a popular news site after visiting a do-it-yourself site, it might make sense to serve up an advert for a hardware store. The hardware store advert on the news site may reinforce an advert that also appeared on the do-it-yourself site. Alternatively, if the news site is proven to get a larger audience of 'do-it-yourselfers' and generate more clicks or conversions, the advert could appear on there instead of the do-it-yourself site.

However, consumers aren't always aware that their online behaviour is being followed. For the most part people do not read the privacy terms and conditions, but that does not mean that they are not concerned about their privacy. Adam Kasper, Director of Digital Media at Media Contacts, has warned that a 'watershed moment' may be coming in the near future. He believes that when consumers gain greater awareness of the extent to which their online activity can be tracked and targeted it may trigger a backlash against behavioural targeting. He says: 'It's the elephant in the room, and there's going to be a point where consumers get it and there's going to be a big public outcry.'

‹ E-mail marketing
New approaches to creative media
> When is offline the best way to advertise online?

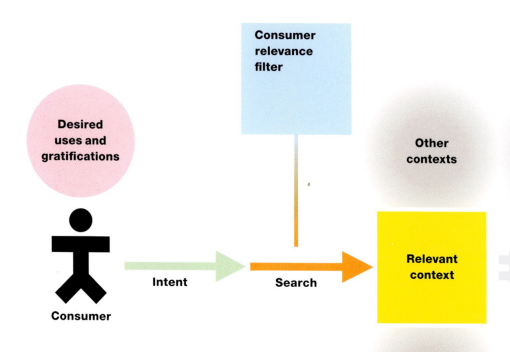

**The role of the contextual
creative brief**
Consumer intent on one side meets
creative messaging on the other side,
via relevant context, facilitated by
the contextual creative brief.

The role of the contextual creative brief

Core business challenge: matching relevant content to relevant context

Relevant content

Contextual creative brief

Potential messages

Advertiser

Key process improvement

When is offline the best way to advertise online?

Interestingly enough, sometimes the best way to generate awareness and traffic online is to advertise offline. This may seem paradoxical until we remember that the Web is typified by its fragmentation, by its ability to gather a vast array of communities around a huge range of websites. While there are a handful of sites that gather extremely large audiences, it is still hard to beat a TV commercial in the right show at the right time for sheer impact and reach. Some of the best examples, both good and bad, come from commercials placed in the highest-rated programme in the US: the Super Bowl.

Mitsubishi

One of the best Super Bowl adverts intended to drive people to a website was for Mitsubishi. In 2004, they ran a simple and effective ad that reached over 41% of all US households at one time. The spot featured a comparison test between a Mitsubishi Galant and the best-selling Toyota Camry. The two cars drove side by side at high speed, each preceded by an 18-wheel truck that started dropping hazards in their way. The cars swerved to avoid flying obstacles such as bowling balls and garbage cans. But the big surprise came when two full-sized sedans came rolling out of the trucks, landed on the road in front of the speeding cars, and started rolling and flipping in front of the two cars. It seemed as if a chain reaction pile-up was just about to begin. Which car would avoid the tremendous collision? Both of them? One of them? Neither of them? Just as the viewer was about to find out, the film froze and a superimposed headline simply stated: <seewhathappens.com>.

According to Ian Beavis, the frank-talking Australian who was Mitsubishi's senior vice president of marketing at the time, 'It bloody near blew the back off the servers!' The numbers were staggering: 31 million visits to <seewhathappens.com> between the Super Bowl and August 2004; 11 million visits within six hours of the broadcast; eight million unique visitors; two-thirds of visitors watched the full commercial twice or more; and web leads to its dealers tripled.

The ad generated more web traffic in 24 hours than <mitsubishi.com> generated in an average month. People spent an inordinate amount of time on the website, which had a consumer pass-along component that went on for weeks after the initial campaign ran.

Hulu

With impact like that it was no surprise that Hulu, the new online video service that offers TV shows, movies and clips, chose 2009's Super Bowl XLIII as the platform to gain broad awareness. To date, nearly 200 content partners have signed on with Hulu, including FOX, NBC Universal, ABC, Comedy Central, Lionsgate, and MTV Networks, to name a few. Over 400 blue chip advertisers have followed suit, including McDonald's, Visa, Best Buy, Johnson & Johnson and Procter & Gamble. Hulu has well over ten million viewers (some estimates claim the figure to be as high as 50 million), and it is growing fast.

Hulu's humorous Super Bowl ad was a key reason for Hulu's popularity with viewers, advertisers and content providers. It positioned Hulu as a tongue-in-cheek evil plot to destroy the world. According to *Adweek*: 'After Hulu debuted its "Alien" ad with Alec Baldwin on the Super Bowl… the site saw a rise of more than 40% in streams.'

✕

<Outpost.com>'s lesson

Just advertising on a high-rated TV show cannot guarantee online success. In the early days of the dot.com boom, <outpost.com>, a highly rated consumer electronics website ran a humorous Super Bowl ad featuring gerbils being fired out of a cannon (trust me, it's funnier than it sounds). Unfortunately, they never clearly explained what the site was for. They expected brand awareness alone to drive visits and sales. Outpost is not around anymore. The basics of great advertising hold true offline and online: people need to know who you are *and* what you do well.

Background

When looking for companies who approach online advertising in a creative manner that makes the most of the unique attributes of the Web, there are few who do it as well as the fast-food brand Burger King (BK) and their advertising agency Crispin Porter + Boguski. They have pioneered a series of innovative and award-winning online campaigns.

Subservient chicken

In 2004, one of BK's first forays into online marketing was the Subservient Chicken campaign, which featured the website <subservientchicken.com> where a man in a chicken suit would do whatever you told him to do when you typed in a command. If you told him to jump; he would jump. If you told him to flap; he would flap. If you got raunchy, however, he would probably wag his finger at you. Now, what does this wacky idea have to do with hamburgers? Well, a lot really. It was a fun way for BK to launch their TenderCrisp chicken sandwich, and to combine it with their brand promise that you could 'have it your way'. When it comes to chicken sandwiches, you are in charge and BK is subservient. The campaign was a monster success. According to a variety of sources, it has had over 20 million unique visitors and upwards of 500 million hits. It may be, as one website calls it, 'the most successful marketing website of all time'.[10]

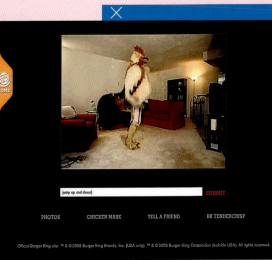

Burger King's Subservient Chicken

Burger King's 'Subservient Chicken' is just one of the many clever and creative advertising approaches that the brand has executed online in the past few years. Any one of BK's web advertising events can be considered gold-standard online marketing. Taken together they are the best of their kind. BK even gave out chicken masks in-store so that life could imitate art.

DIRECTIONS
1. Cut along dotted line.
2. Put on chicken face.
3. Be subservient.

< When is offline the best way to advertise online?
Case study: Burger King become online innovators
> Questions and exercises

Whopper virgins

In 2008, BK launched a unique and somewhat controversial eight-minute documentary-style Internet film. The film was shot in remote parts of Thailand, Greenland and Romania. It documented people who had never eaten a hamburger trying their first BK Whopper and taste-testing it against McDonald's Big Mac. Watching people eat their first hamburger is an oddly fascinating experience for the viewer, and soon you forget you are watching a commercial. You become caught up in the lives of these people, and how their culture and cuisine is having a greater impact on the film crew than the hamburger is on them. The website offers only one option aside from watching the film. A button labelled 'share'. The film's controversy arises from the feeling, by many, that perhaps these remote people would have been better off without the 'blessings' of hamburgers and crass commercialism. However, there is no denying that the 'Whopper Virgins' campaign is very engaging.

Whopper freak out

In 2009, BK won the coveted Grand Effie award for their 'Whopper freak out' integrated campaign which featured TV adverts that drove people to the Web to see another eight-minute documentary film. This film featured an experiment in which BK took its much-loved Whopper off the menu without warning and filmed customers to see what would happen. In stage two of the experiment, they removed the Whopper and replaced it with competing burgers. As you might expect, Whopper lovers freaked out, which made for an entertaining film, underscoring how much people loved the taste of their Whopper. Carl Johnson, Chairman of the Board of Directors of the Effie awards, said, 'Burger King won the Grand Effie convincingly due to their boldness and creativity across multiple media platforms, delivering real cultural relevance and above all, outstanding business results.'

Whopper sacrifice

BK also had another great online idea that got cut short. In 2008, in order to take advantage of the popularity of social networking, BK created the Whopper Sacrifice campaign. The campaign, which was a Facebook application, offered a free whopper for every ten Facebook friends or contacts that you were willing to sacrifice. The 'sacrificed' contacts would receive an e-mail notifying them that they had been ditched for a Whopper. Facebook, however, decided that the promotion didn't meet its business philosophy and BK shut it down after just a week, but not before they had already attracted over 80,000 users.

Question 1
Burger King has created a number of eight-minute documentary-style videos. What are the advantages and disadvantages of online videos of this length?

Question 2
If you were the marketing director of Burger King, what kind of online idea would you try next? Try to think of something that no one has done before. Be creative!

Questions and exercises

>

Discussion questions

1

Bob Garfield's prognosis for traditional advertising agencies in the digital age is somewhat dire (see page 74). What specific steps do you think advertising agencies need to take to evolve and survive?

2

In your experience, what is the most creative use of advertising you have seen on the Web? Is there something you have seen online that was unforgettable and branded at the same time?

3

Of the branded entertainment you see on the Web, what percentage of them do you pass on to other people? What percentage do you receive from friends by e-mail that you feel are good enough to continue passing on?

Exercises

1

Pick one of your favourite products. Write a display ad for it using the suggestions for 'writing display ads for the Web' on page 77. Think about how it might be different as a skyscraper ad versus a rectangle ad.

2

In groups, try to develop a viral idea that you can put on YouTube that will be good enough for people to share with others. If the idea is good enough, shoot it, post it, share it and see what happens!

3

List some specific ways by which a local restaurant in your neighbourhood could take advantage of geographical and behavioural targeting to increase its traffic.

4

Herman Miller Inc. is the office furniture company that created the hugely popular Aeron chair (if you haven't seen one, look it up online). Write a contextual creative brief that identifies the best reason to buy one (there are many, but what's the best?) and the best context for the message (where would people be most receptive to the message – online or offline?).

Summary

Online advertising is a field that is developing rapidly. The days of creating static banner ads (the equivalent of a print ad on the net) are coming to a close. Web ads are becoming deep, dynamic, functional and connected. Extended-length advertising content and viral advertising online are now commonplace. Online targeting is becoming a subtle art. The tracking and data-collection functions of the Web allow for finely tuned geographic and behavioural advertising approaches. Online advertising is now more varied in its potential approaches to audiences and content than all other traditional media vehicles combined.

Suggested further reading

Plummer, J., Rappaport S., Hall, T., and Barocci, R. 2007. *The Online Advertising Playbook: Proven Strategies and Tested Tactics from the Advertising Research Foundation.* Hoboken: John Wiley & Sons, Inc.

Godin, S. 1999. *Permission Marketing: Turning Strangers Into Friends And Friends Into Customers.* New York: Simon & Schuster

Endnotes

1
ZenithOptimedia. Retrieved from <paidcontent.org> (10 April 2010)

2
Keane, M. (posted 30 June 2009). 'OPA launches new ad formats to help the display market'. Retrieved from <www.econsultancy.com> (10 April 2010)

3
Keane, M. (posted 19 June 2009) 'Bringing the reign of click-throughs to an end'. Retrieved from <www.econsultancy.com> (10 April 2010)

4
Advertising Age (posted 15 June 2009) 'You won't believe who's behind these viral videos'. Retrieved 19 April 2010

5
Donahue, S. (27 May 2009). 'Ideal length for Internet video ads: 40 seconds'. Retrieved from <www.contentinople.com> (10 April 2010)

6
Carlson, N. (28 November 2008). 'Hulu users choose two minute ads'. Retrieved from <www.businessinsider.com> (1 November 2010)

7 and 9
Dru, J.M. (2002). *Beyond Disruption: Changing the Rules in the Marketplace.* New York: John Wiley and Sons, Inc.

8
Schumann, D.W. and Thorson, E (2007). *Internet Advertising: Theory and Practice.* New Jersey: Lawrence Erlbaum Associates

10
The Barbarian Group: Portfolio. Retrieved from <www.barbariangroup.com> (5 February 2010)

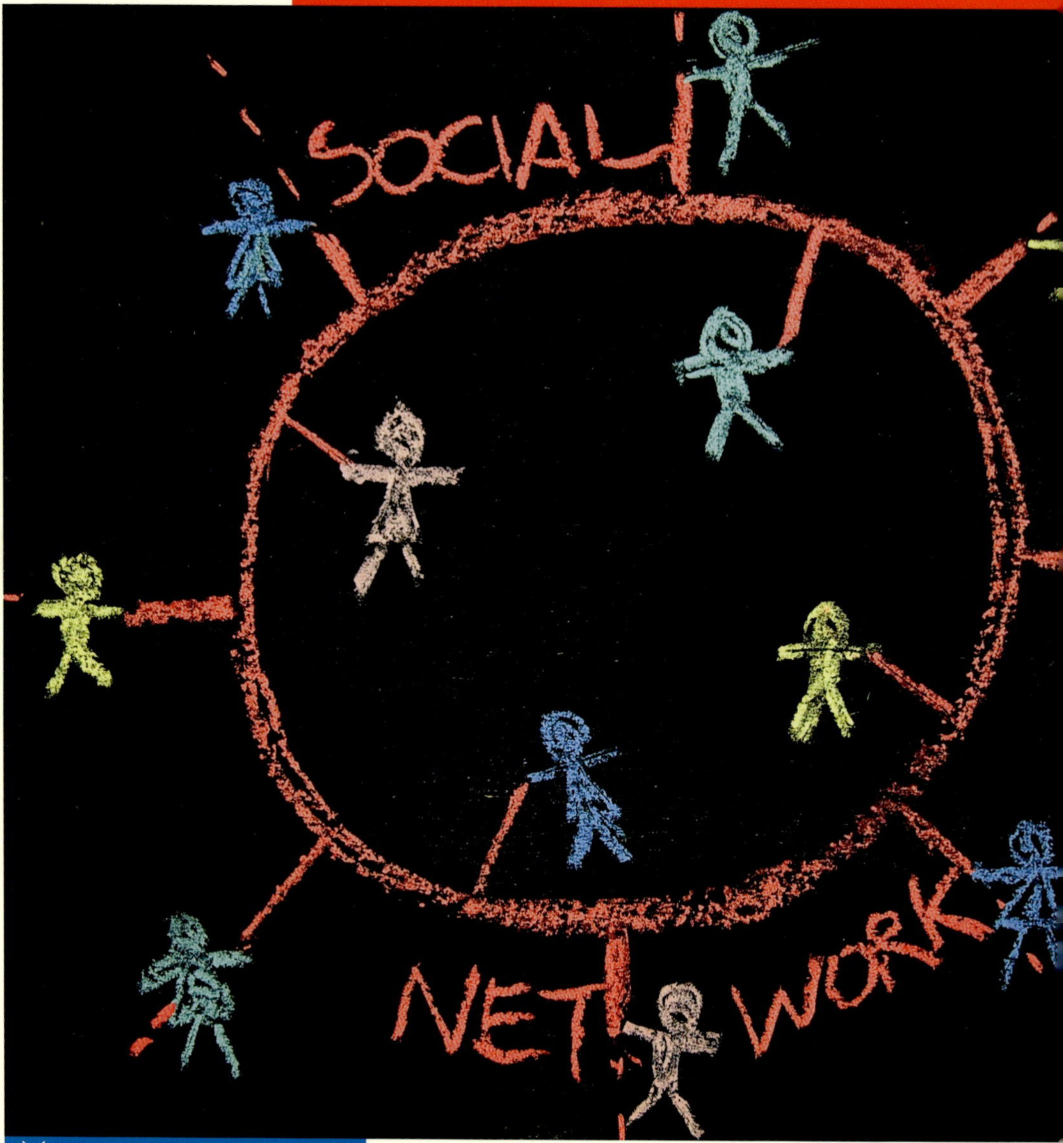
SOCIAL
NETWORK

This chapter looks at one of the most exciting recent developments in online marketing: the emergence of online social communities powered by consumers. We will see how social connections are reshaping the way people interact with their world, and the way they make decisions about which products they buy.

Social web connections take many forms. We will look closely at blogs, wikis, social networks and virtual social worlds. The chapter ends with one of the most successful, and surprising, social marketing success stories: Barack Obama's presidential campaign.

The rise of social networks
Social networking has taken online marketing, and the world, by storm. Today, marketers need to have a strategy for engaging online communities of like-minded people in a relevant way.

〈

European society in the Middle Ages was divided into three clear categories: clergy, nobility and commoners. These were known as the three 'estates'. In the early 19th century, the emergence of the press as a check on those in power led to the press being referred to as 'the fourth estate'. Since then, the term 'the fifth estate' has been bandied about to describe various groups in society, everything from fraternal organisations to trade unions to crime syndicates. In reality, the term currently has no fixed meaning.

When we consider the incredible potential of people when they are digitally connected to each other, the social web may someday be considered the true fifth estate. Its claim to such elevated status is due in part to its ability to transfer power to common people. In part, it is due to the social web's ability to challenge the traditional press as a source of news, information and decision-making. The social web's impact on society is so significant that it deserves to be viewed through the lens of historical significance.

Blogs

Blog is short for 'web log'. Blogs were one of the earliest forms of social networking on the Web. Originally, most blogs were nothing more than individuals posting their opinions to a website, like an online diary. What made them unique was that many blogs allowed their readers to post their comments too, which started an ongoing conversation between the blog writer and their audience, and between audience members.

Today, the most popular blogs on the Internet have become specialised, almost like interactive online magazines or newspapers. People visit certain blogs when they are interested in learning about specific subjects. In the US, one of the most visited blogs is *The Huffington Post*. Started by American socialite Arianna Huffington in 2005, *The Huffington Post* has become a top destination for political news. *The Observer* newspaper of London named it 'the most powerful blog in the world'. Opinions posted on *The Huffington Post* have a power to shape opinion and public policy once reserved for the likes of *The New York Times*, *TIME* magazine and *The Economist*.

The Huffington Post
Some blogs are now as well respected as newspapers. The liberal-leaning blog, *The Huffington Post*, has translated its opinions and online conversations into real political power.

Blogs come in all shapes and sizes. There are blogs in every country about every subject imaginable. If you live in Australia and you are interested in gadgets and technology, visit <www.gizmodo.com.au>. Do you live in South Africa and love rugby? Visit <www.keo.co.za>. It is estimated that there have been over 130 million blogs put up on the Web since 2002. About 350 million people read blogs. Seventy per cent of active Internet users read blogs. And there are almost one million blog posts every 24 hours.[1]

Influencing blogs and the influence of blogs

From a marketing perspective, the growing popularity of blogs is important for two reasons. First, blogs are influencing consumers' purchase behaviour. Increasingly, people are checking blogs to see what is being said about the products that they intend to buy. If a popular blog recommends a specific product, more people will buy it. Secondly, many blogs sell ad space and have become important advertising vehicles in their own right. Buying ad space on many blogs is easy, and often reasonably priced.

Influencing blogs to say good things about your products is harder. Marketers use many strategies to influence **bloggers**, including simple strategies like sending press releases to the blogger and/or blog contributors. A more sophisticated approach is to create an ongoing relationship with selected blogs. For example, companies often send their products to relevant bloggers on a regular basis, asking them to write up their opinions about them. If the products are good, they get great reviews. If not, they get valuable criticism that helps to improve them.

Sony, for example, launched a programme called 'DigiDads', which placed its products with a small group of blogging dads in the hope that they would play with them and write good things about them. Beyond buying ads or influencing reviews, companies need to think about getting directly involved in blog conversations. One way to do this is for the company or product to create its own blog. Another is to post comments on the most popular and influential blogs covering your business. Many marketers try both of these approaches.

Another strategy is to let your employees blog about their areas of expertise. Hewlett-Packard, for example, has a site called 'HP employee business blogs', which includes almost a dozen employee blogs covering subjects such as digital photography, business-driven IT management and gaming. But employee blogging is a double-edged sword. It is not always easy to control. It raises issues of confidentiality and legal liability. Sun Microsystems, for example, encourages its employees to blog, but it also sets clear guidelines about what not to do, including speculation, disclosing confidential information and revealing personal information. They make it clear that irresponsible blogging can cost Sun dearly and may even cost the blogger their job.

Marketers in sheep's clothing

One of the most egregious mistakes any marketer can make is to post messages to a blog without identifying them as coming from the company in question. Some companies have stupidly tried to influence the conversation on blogs by posing as informed consumers. Their belief was that if people knew the information was coming from the company in question, they would ignore it, or consider it to be propaganda. Unfortunately, marketers who get caught posing as consumers end up losing far more ground with real consumers than they ever hoped to gain.

Similarly, some marketers have paid bloggers to write positive things without openly disclosing the relationship. In the long run, this hurts the company's credibility as well as the blogger's. In 2003, for example, soft drink maker Dr Pepper/7-Up approached teenage bloggers to hype their new milk-based drink, named 'Raging Cow', but they did not want the bloggers to divulge the relationship. The arrangement created a backlash. At least one boycott was proposed, and Dr Pepper/7-Up had to publicly admit that it would do things better next time. Raging Cow did get lots of mentions and awareness, but much of the buzz was negative.

Running glossary

bloggers
people who complete web logs (blogs) or who regularly publish an online diary

In the United States in 2009 the Federal Trade Commission (FTC), the government organisation that protects consumers from fraud, instituted new guidelines requiring bloggers to disclose any 'material connection' to an advertiser. Material connection includes payments or free products. Indicative of the fundamental changes wrought by the digital media revolution, this was the first time that the FTC had updated its rules on endorsements in advertising for almost 30 years.

Wikis

The term wiki comes from the Hawaiian word for 'fast'. Wikis are websites that use special software designed to allow people to collaborate in building the site's content. They allow users to edit existing content as well as to upload new content. The results are sites that reflect the best efforts of often thousands or even millions of people, rather than the work of a few specialists. It is quite literally an 'open source' approach.

Wikis have the potential to transform both the workplace and economic production. Don Tapscott and Anthony Williams coined this idea and its name 'wikinomics', in 2006. Eric Schmidt, Google CEO, noted: 'Wikinomics heralds the biggest change in collaboration to date. Thanks to the Internet, masses of people outside the boundaries of traditional hierarchies can innovate to produce content, goods and services.'[2]

The most famous and successful wiki is Wikipedia, the free online encyclopaedia. We'll take a closer look at the inner workings of Wikipedia because it embodies the promise and potential problems of wikis.

Wikipedia

Wikipedia was not the first online encyclopaedia. In fact its founder, Jimmy Wales, started a failed one in 2000 called 'Nupedia'. Nupedia failed for the same reason that many early online projects failed: it tried to replicate traditional media online (in this case, the printed encyclopaedia) instead of taking advantage of the unique attributes and possibilities of the Web. Nupedia, for example, used the same model for developing its content as regular encyclopaedias did. They had the requisite academics, peer review, editing and so on. Over a year and a half later, after an expenditure of $250,000 (£165,000), they had a grand total of only 12 articles!

Wikipedia is something entirely different. It was created by millions of users sharing their knowledge. Wikipedia has three basic rules:

1

Information must develop from a *neutral point of view* (it should not be selling a specific political, religious or commercial point of view).

2

Information should be *verifiable* (it must be supported by published sources).

3

Information should *not be based on original research* (it must be supported by existing research).

Wikipedia doesn't make these rules prerequisites or filters, as that might limit the level of contribution. Although the information posted is not always initially correct, Wikipedia believes it becomes correct over time, by a combination of contributors correcting faulty information and Wikipedia's own ongoing efforts to spot-check information after the fact. Wikipedia takes down spot-checked information that does not meet its criteria. According to Wikipedia's Jimmy Wales, 'We could be draconian about how we police the site, but that's like throwing everyone in jail for any minor infraction…. We'd rather try to build a healthy, positive environment so people feel positively inclined to contribute in a constructive way.'

Wikipedia's supporters are confident that Wikipedia can fix itself on an ongoing basis when faulty information is input.

In a nutshell, Wikipedia's approach means that the site has the benefit of more than just a few experts; it has the combined knowledge of millions of people. James Surowiecki outlined the essentials necessary to create combined knowledge in his influential book *The Wisdom of Crowds*. A 'wise crowd' must be diverse, so that lots of different opinions are represented. It must be decentralised so that no single influencer can direct the outcome. It must be independent, so that 'good' information can balance out 'bad' information. Finally, it must be collaborative, so that it can result in 'collective intelligence'. Wikipedia is all of these things.

Despite Wikipedia's ability to 'heal itself' when false information is posted, it is impossible to know, at any given point in time, if the information posted is entirely correct. For that reason, some have called Wikipedia a 'representation of knowledge' as opposed to knowledge itself.[3] Like any form of social networking, it is made strong by its connectivity, but its veracity is essentially only as good as its weakest link.

Imagine a world in which every single person on the planet is given free access to the sum of all human knowledge. That's what we're doing.

Jimmy Wales
Wikipedia founder

Crowdsourcing

Wikis go way beyond Wikipedia. Their open-source collaboration potential has many marketing applications. Instead of conducting surveys or focus group research to find out what people want, wiki software enables companies to let their customers help them actually create the next generation of products or solve brand marketing problems. This ability to gather large groups of people around your brand and get them working to develop products and/or solutions is called **crowdsourcing**.

Crowdsourcing is quick, productive and cheap. The world's largest advertiser, Procter & Gamble, uses a site called <innocentive.com> to connect with a crowd of over 140,000 scientists and engineers worldwide to solve research and development dilemmas for their products. Even NASA uses crowdsourcing.

They have found it ten times faster to use online crowds to measure craters on images of Mars. NASA calls their contributors 'clickworkers', and they work for free.

For example, advertising agencies have even begun to lose business to crowdsourcing. Unilever, one of the world's biggest advertisers, recently fired the London-based agency working on their Peperami meat snack brand. Unilever is offering $10,000 (approximately £6,700) to the winner of a competition to develop new TV and print advertising ideas.

Bob Seelert, author of *Start with the Answer: And Other Wisdom for Aspiring Leaders*, believes this trend will only go so far because concentrated expertise will always be valued. Regarding advertising agencies, he says: 'If you told me that [crowdsourcing is] going to be the outsourcing of everything the agency does to some outside group of people… connected via the Internet, who haven't really worked over the course of a long period of time to understand the equity of the brand and how to bring it to life with consumers in a professional way. I'd say I don't believe that's happening at all.'

> [The agency] has done great work over the years. They've created a strong creative vehicle that's extremely well defined and portable. But their great work has created a problem for them, because it makes Peperami the obvious candidate for crowdsourcing.

Matt Burgess
Managing Director
Unilever

Social media challenges Iran's state-controlled media

The power of social media is indeed profound. Its potential as a marketing medium only tells a small part of the story. For many of the same reasons that social media is changing the way that companies look at consumers, it is also changing the political landscape. Nowhere has that been more evident than in Iran.

In June 2009, Iranian President Mahmoud Ahmadinejad defeated Mir-Hossein Mousavi to win re-election in a controversial election result that led to large-scale protests and demonstrations.

Iran's theocratic leadership is noted for its tight control of the media. In the past, protest against the government usually went unreported, especially outside of Iran. However, with the advent of social media, these recent election protests were very different. While the official media was largely silent, Twitter, Facebook, blogs and so on, got the news out. Major broadcasters' headlines about the state of affairs in Iran on BBC and CNN came not from reporters, but directly from the Twitter feeds and Facebook postings of average Iranians.

A central image that served as a rallying cry for the protesters was a video of the brutal death of a young girl named 'Neda'. The video was posted to Facebook and then placed on YouTube. It led to an explosion of Twitter discussion about her death, which galvanised support and led to more protests worldwide. Neda in Farsi means 'voice'.

Running glossary

crowdsourcing
the practice of tapping into the creativity of a large crowd of enthusiasts, often using wiki software, to collaborate in the design of new products or in solving marketing questions

Social networks are the fastest growing phenomenon on the Web, and the one that will most fundamentally change marketing as we know it. Two-thirds of the world's Internet population visit them. In highly developed markets, the percentage is even higher. In the UK, for example, the number is 80%. According to a survey by Anderson Analytics in the US, 71% of social network users said they could not live without them. Social networking is so popular that users now spend more time on social networks and blogs than they do on e-mail; and people now share twice as much content on Facebook as they do via e-mail.[4] Social networks are growing three times faster than Internet use as a whole and now account for 10% of all online activity.

Two of the most popular social networks are MySpace and Facebook. Facebook in particular has seen tremendous growth worldwide. How fast is it growing? Well, Facebook hit 175 million users just five weeks after it hit 150 million. People spend over three billion minutes on Facebook every day. There are also specialised social sites like LinkedIn (business connections) and Digg (sharing news).

Harnessing social networks

Unsurprisingly, marketers have tried to make the most of this new medium. Pizza Hut, for example, created a Facebook application enabling users to order a Pizza without leaving the site. The British website, <getthemin.com>, which facilitates gift giving, allows Facebook users to buy virtual drinks for their friends which can be cashed in for real drinks at participating UK stores. Not to be outdone, the Canadian division of Dove beauty products created a Facebook application called *Pay Beauty Forward*, which, to date, has allowed over 15,000 friends to send e-flowers to each other with messages like 'You're beautiful!'.

Social networks are places that people go to talk to their friends and acquaintances. These sites are creating a fundamental challenge to traditional marketing. On one level, they take time away from traditional media. On another level, they have changed the way that consumers hear about, learn about and decide about which products they buy. Here is how *BusinessWeek* describes the change:

'Word of mouth – peer opinion – has consistently been rated the most credible source of information. But traditionally there's been a limit as to how widely you could distribute a friend's point of view.... Three decades ago, telling a lot of friends wasn't nearly as easy as it is now. Credibility now has a channel for mass distribution. It's called the Web and it particularly thrives in social networks.'

Social pass-along increases credibility

Credibility really is the name of the game. As product and brand information from social networks is increasingly perceived as more credible, traditional forms of mass messaging become relatively less credible. The Chief Marketing Officer (CMO) council estimates that 15% of major global corporations now monitor online word of mouth.

Credibility is only one problem facing marketers. Another is the issue of how to use social networks to build brands. Social networks are essentially about connecting with friends. People may learn about products from their friends while they are there, but that is not why they are there.

Facebook active users (millions)
Social networking on the Web is expanding at an amazing rate. Facebook hit 175 million users only five weeks after it hit 150 million.

Facebook active users (millions)

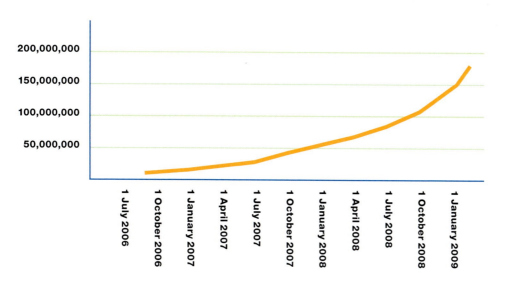

Advertising on social networks

Social networks are not necessarily a great platform to place advertising, and the advertising that does exist is easy to ignore. If it becomes too intrusive, people will go elsewhere to connect with their friends. Despite the fact that thousands of brands have created their own Facebook pages, most of them get little traffic.

Marketers may need to reframe the challenge away from advertising on social networks and towards influencing the conversations on social networks. Marketers such as 7-Eleven monitor online social conversations, which is called 'text mining'. By mining these conversations, 7-Eleven was able to develop a campaign for their iced coffee that was more in tune with consumers' attitudes. Stephanie Hoppe, 7-Eleven's senior director of marketing, believes this leads to better campaigns both online and offline: 'It's not in a focus-group setting so we were getting explicit and authentic data,' Ms Hoppe said. 'It helped us create an effective campaign that was a little out of the norm for us.'

Another major way marketers are taking advantage of social networks is by using the unique aspects of Twitter.

Twitter is a unique social network that not only connects friends but also allows individuals to stream messages to those people who want to 'follow' them. In many ways, Twitter has transformed social networking into micro-blogging.

Users are limited to messages of 140 characters to describe to their followers 'what they are doing now'. These micro-broadcasts are called 'tweets'. Depending on how many followers you have, your tweets may be able to influence a lot of people. In some extreme cases, such as with mega-celebrities, the reach of a person's Twitter feed can challenge traditional broadcast media.

Celebrities such as Britney Spears, Ashton Kutcher and Oprah Winfrey each claim to have more than one million Twitter followers. According to Kutcher, 'One man can have a voice that's as loud as an entire media company.' Actors, singers and other celebrities have capitalised on Twitter's no-cost production to build their brands and connect directly with their audience. Previously, they relied on middle-men to get to their consumers (such as the press, movie studios or record companies). This underscores the fact that social-web marketing, when done well, can have a very high return at an extremely low cost.

Twitter acts as a short broadcast feed rather than just a social destination, and brands such as Dunkin' Donuts have taken full advantage. Their communications manager, Dave Puner, is better known on Twitter as 'Dunkin' Dave'. People follow Dave just because they like his light-hearted, genial tweets. They are fun! Similarly, Pizza Hut gained notice when it advertised to hire summer 'Twinterns' to be their voice on Twitter.

Razorfish, a top interactive advertising agency, notes that consumers have been lukewarm to current social media efforts by marketers. They recommend that social media should be core to brand communications strategy, as opposed to being an afterthought. If not, says Shiv Singh, vice president of global social media at Razorfish, 'it's a recipe for disaster'.

Social networks, however, still need to prove that they can be both profitable and effective as advertising vehicles. Many marketers are highly sceptical about the effectiveness of display ads on social networks. If they hope to make significant money from advertisers, the networks themselves will need to find creative new ways to connect advertisers and consumers without undermining the very reason for their existence. Twitter, for example, is experimenting with sponsored tweets. The news is not all bad, however. An eye tracking study by Oneupweb showed that people do notice ads on social network sites. According to Oneupweb's director of operations, Tim Kauffold, 'There's not blindness toward ads in social networks. People still look at the ads.'

Whether social networks will be an effective tool for marketers to reach lots of consumers with their advertising messages is still questionable. Perhaps the best advice comes from a report by Knowledge Networks, which recommends that sites such as Twitter are 'less a way to directly reach customers, and more a way to reach passionate voices who may influence perceptions of your brand'.

A passing fancy?

The incredible growth of online social networks, combined with the high levels of enthusiasm they have engendered in their users, bodes well for their long-term survival. However, as with any trend, there is a chance that social networking fatigue could set in. Some worry that social networks will transform from a long term game-changing trend into a short-term fad.

It is most likely that dominant social networks, such as Facebook, will someday be replaced by new sites with newer features, just as Facebook and Myspace buried their predecessor, Friendster. What is highly unlikely is that consumers will stop using digital means to keep in touch with friends, family and acquaintances. Online social networks are now a fixture, like e-mail. And like e-mail before it, although it has its frustrations, it is still a form of communication we no longer want to live without.

Another way to interact socially on the Web is to do so virtually. Virtual networking takes many forms. Two of the most popular are virtual worlds, such as Second Life, and massively multiplayer online role-playing games (MMORPGs), such as World of Warcraft.

Virtual networks inject a large dose of fantasy into the social equation by allowing people to represent themselves online with computer-generated characters called avatars. Avatars sometimes look like the actual users they represent. Just as often, they are fictional representations.

In the Second Life website people live in a complete virtual world. Users are called 'residents', and they can socialise with other residents, take part in activities and do just about anything they can do in real life. They can buy homes, cars and services. They can even sell things. Second Life has therefore become very popular with marketers. Many have created virtual storefronts or other brand manifestations. For big brands, it is a chance to reinforce their dominance in the real world with a significant presence in the virtual one. For smaller brands, it may be a chance to gain an edge by having a big presence in a place that their bigger competitors may not have.

A good example of the marriage between marketing and virtual worlds is Habbo, a teen-based virtual world that has over 11 million monthly users worldwide. They joined with the cosmetics brand Coty to launch the singer Gwen Stephani's 'Harajuku Lovers' fragrance. The programme featured the new perfume in an in-world room called 'The Harajuku Lovers Hub', where users (called 'Habbos') interact in surroundings inspired by Tokyo's funky Harajuku district.

One of the most popular and important social environments online is multiplayer gaming. There are now many MMORPGs that allow a huge numbers of people to play together, each person playing a role in the game using an avatar. The undisputed king of MMORPGs is World of Warcraft (WOW). WOW is estimated to have over 60% of the MMORPG market. It has over ten million monthly subscribers! WOW is a game where you can fight monsters, interact with other players, and complete quests, together or separately. With a monthly fee of $14.99/£9.99, WOW is one of the few social sites that makes lots of money.

SimpsonizeMe

In the previous chapter, we talked about the effectiveness of well-crafted viral videos. Social interaction is the key to viral success, as people feel compelled to share these videos with friends via e-mail and social networking sites. In this chapter, we have talked about the social opportunities created by avatars in virtual worlds. In 2007 for the launch of *The Simpsons Movie* (the movie version of the popular animated TV series) Fox studios and Burger King teamed up to take advantage of social connectivity and the popularity of avatars.

Fox created a website, called SimpsonizeMe, where users could upload their picture and have it transformed into an animated Simpsons-like character. For Simpsons fans, it was irresistible to see what they would look like as one of their characters. Once you saw it, and laughed, the website let you send it to your network of friends.

After the launch of SimpsonizeMe, many people used their characters as their official Facebook or Myspace pictures. Others pinned them up in their school lockers or in their office. By 2008, the site still had monthly traffic of almost 300,000. In 2009, it was still Burger King's third most visited site globally. The site also helped the movie succeed at the box office. The film earned over $30 million (£20 million) on its opening day and $74 million (£49 million) on its opening weekend. It was the third highest non-sequel opening of all time. For a July opening of a non-sequel, it was number one of all time.

Avatars, social networks and the Simpsons made for a potent combination. Skittles, a brand never far behind on social-web trends, recently launched a similar application called 'Go Skittle Yourself'.

Engaged consumers

Many marketers see a big opportunity in gaming due to its high level of involvement. Skittles fruit candies, for example, created a branded role-playing game in the UK where avatars can battle each other in a series of 'skuffles', with the ultimate goal of getting other members to become fans of your avatar. MMORPGs can also be the backdrop for ads, as in a US Toyota Tacoma truck ad where the truck became a dominant weapon in World of Warcraft.

The benefits of virtual marketing are very real. According to a 2006 study sponsored by IBM and Seriosity, Inc., and executed by professors at Stanford and MIT, the average online gamer is young (27 years old), spends huge amounts of time playing online (22 hours a week on average), and is willing to spend money to acquire virtual assets and expertise (over $1 billion/£660 million per year). For many marketers, young, engaged consumers who are willing to spend money are a primary target, or often *the* primary target.

Pitfalls: Skittles

We have seen that the marketers of Skittles fruit candies are extremely innovative when it comes to social networking ideas. However, they learned the hard way that these ideas can sometimes backfire. In early 2009, Skittles turned control of their home page over to the people by connecting it directly to Twitter. Every time there was a Skittles reference on Twitter, it showed up on the site. Unfortunately, they did this with no process of review or editing. Twitter's Skittles references suddenly began to include such things as profanity and statements mocking the brand. They were forced to take down the site the very next day.

Skittles, in their effort to give online social network users more involvement, learned a key lesson about social media: a brand needs to engage people and actively engage in discussions with people, not just hand over control and step aside.

Successful social-web marketing

Advertising Agency Universal McCann published a global 'Power to the People' study. In it, they offer a number of important tips for successful social-web marketing. Among them:

- Make the experience better when shared
- Give users something to join
- Refresh content regularly

Larry Weber, in his book *Marketing to the Social Web*, outlines an even more comprehensive seven-step process for marketers to get it right:

1
Observe
Find the most influential online places where people congregate, listen to what they are saying and map it.

2
Recruit
Enlist a core group of people who want to talk about your product.

3
Evaluate platforms
Is your best opportunity to enter the conversation on an existing blog, your own blog, a social network, somewhere else or a combination of places?

4
Engage
This is about content. What content will get people visiting, sharing, talking and responding?

5
Measure
Define success. Create measures to track your progress.

6
Promote
Get the word out about your online content, both online and offline.

7
Improve
Make it better. Make it better. Then make it better again.

Case study: Barack Obama's election campaign

Background

What can the President of the United States teach big brands about how to execute effective social-network marketing? A lot. In fact, Barack Obama's online marketing savvy was the key reason that he was named *Advertising Age* magazine's 2008 'Marketer of the Year', and won both the Integrated Grand Prix and the Titanium Grand Prix awards at the prestigious Cannes Advertising Festival. (The Titanium award goes to the most breakthrough concept of the year.) For a politician – as opposed to a product, service or charity – to win, or even be mentioned for these awards, was absolutely groundbreaking.

Obama's success was due both to the reach of his campaign and its social connectivity. Although he was trying to win an election in America, he built a fan following worldwide over the Internet. The online campaign enabled users and visitors to get involved, share and contribute. Prasoon Joshi, McCann Erickson's executive chairman India, and regional creative director of Asia, was on the Cannes jury. He noted that, 'Obama was a brand created by the consumer, along with the brand owner.'

Social media campaign

The Obama online social-media campaign was masterful. His team followed Weber's seven-step process to the letter. In particular, they keenly observed their target audience, figuring out the key places online that were the most influential for an average American's election decision making. They recruited people online and engaged them so well that many started working actively to drum up support for the campaign. And they had a clear conduit strategy. It was so clear that the emerging media magazine, *Contagious*, observed that, 'His team blogged, Twittered and YouTubed their way to a win.'

The campaign was extremely well integrated. Each piece was infused with the core campaign idea: 'Change'. And each piece trumpeted the empowering slogan, 'Yes, we can!' Obama had presence in every major social-media forum imaginable, including Facebook, MySpace, Twitter, Digg, Flickr, LinkedIn, Blackplanet and many more. Videos, messages, speeches and campaign information were posted to these sites daily, and Twittered. They even created a branded application for the iPhone with a 'Call Your Friend' feature, which organised your contacts by swing state, so that you could specifically target the friends who would make the most difference on election day.

Local activism and small donations

The centrepiece of the campaign was a social networking site called <mybarackobama.com>. Obama's team even hired one of Facebook's founders to run it. Ultimately, it connected 13 million Americans with the campaign and with each other. <Mybarackobama.com> let people volunteer in their communities, make donations, organise online discussions and upload their own artwork and videos. As a result, Obama created more local community support, rallied more volunteers and raised more money than any candidate in history. While both presidential candidates relied on big donors, Obama had a huge advantage in the form of small donations from the millions of everyday people with whom his campaign had connected.

The seeds for Obama's online success were actually sown in the 2004 presidential campaign of Howard Dean. Dean, a Democrat, shocked his opponents with his ability to use the Web to raise significant sums of money and rally local activism on his behalf.

Question 1
How has selling products and services become more like politics in the digital age?

Question 2
<Mybarackobama.com> is still an active site. Visit it and discuss whether the Obama online campaign is taking lessons from brands that try to build long-term equity.

After that election, Dean became chairman of the Democratic National Committee, whose major role was to help get Democrats, including Barack Obama, elected. *The New York Observer* attributed Obama's election to perfecting the online approaches that Dean had pioneered four years before.

We all know that Barack Obama won. But he did not just win; he won in a landslide. It seems marketers have quite a lot to learn from the President of the United States.

Questions and exercises

>

Discussion questions

1

Do you think that advertising will be an effective method for social networks to turn a profit? If not, how much do you think they could charge without losing too many people?

2

Why do you think that most universities do not accept Wikipedia as a reliable source for research papers?

3

What should Obama do in 2012 to improve the way he reaches online communities via social network sites?

Exercises

1

Visit *The Huffington Post*. Have a debate. One side should argue that it is a political blog. The other side should argue that it is entertainment media. What does this debate tell you about online convergence?

2

Imagine that you are the marketing director for Weight Watchers' low-calorie meals. What online communities would you want to influence? Surf the Web and map the places that people congregate around dieting. Which are the most visited? Which are the most influential?

3

Visit <secondlife.com>. If you were a new mobile phone brand, what opportunities would you have to get recognition in the virtual world that you might not be able to afford in the real world? List your three biggest ideas.

4

Look at your Facebook page or someone else's. Look at the small ads. Do you think that they work? Try to design an advertising approach that would be more effective without being too annoying.

Summary

No development on the Web is having a bigger impact currently than the emergence of social media. Social media is not just one phenomenon. It is an amalgam of many new aspects of the Web including blogs, microblogs, wikis, social networks, crowdsourcing, multiplayer online games and more. Marketers who use social networking to build brands or sell products need to be very careful in their approach. They need to make sure that they are adding value to the social experience and not just trying to exploit it. They also need to be open and honest in their approaches, never concealing their true intentions or identity.

Suggested further reading

Safko, L. and Brake, D. K. 2009. *The Social Media Bible: Tactics, Tools & Strategies for Business Success.* Hoboken: John Wiley & Sons, Inc.

Weber, L. 2009. *Marketing to the Social Web: How Digital Customer Communities Build Your Business*, 2nd ed. Hoboken: John Wiley & Sons, Inc.

Bruns, A. 2008. *Blogs, Wikipedia, Second Life, and Beyond.* New York: Peter Lang Publishing, Inc.

Tapscott, D. and Williams, A. D. 2008. *Wikinomics: How Mass Collaboration Changes Everything.* New York: Portfolio

Surowiecki, J. 2005. *The Wisdom of Crowds.* New York: Anchor Books

Endnotes

1
Singer, A. (8 March 2010). 'Architecting a social web marketing and PR strategy'. Retrieved from <www.thefuturebuzz.com> (19 April 2010)

2
Tapscott, D. and Williams, A. D. 2008. *Wikinomics: How Mass Collaboration Changes Everything.* New York: Portfolio

3
Bruns, A. 2008. *Blogs, Wikipedia, Second Life, and Beyond.* New York: Peter Lang Publishing, Inc.

4
Maher, R. (26 February 2010). 'Forget email, Facebook is where people share content'. Retrieved from <www.businessinsider.com> (3 March 2010)

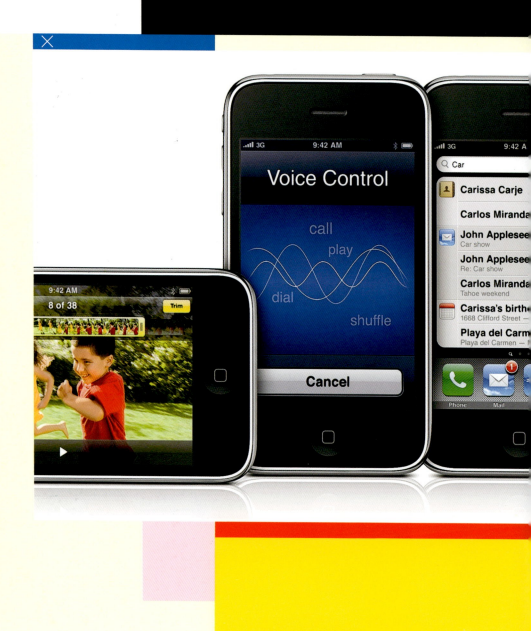

This chapter looks at the liberation of digital media from the confines of computers and computer hard drives. We will look at how 'cloud computing' is helping to make computers smaller, cheaper and more portable. We will then look at how programming applications that help deliver new online functionality are creating a revolution in interactive marketing and mobile telephony.

The current period has been called by some the 'late early stage of the mobile web'.[1] The exciting marketing examples we will look at in this chapter are just the beginning of a digital movement that promises to rival the early days of the Internet in terms of its explosive growth and increasing lifestyle benefits to consumers worldwide.

iPhone apps have produced a wave of online innovation
Online applications have opened up a new wave of growth and development for the Web, and for mobile platforms in particular, thanks to devices like Apple's iPhone.

There is a quiet revolution taking hold on the Internet. Where once computers were loaded with lots of memory and built-in software, developers are now taking full advantage of the Web's immense storage capabilities. Using the Web to host information that can be accessed from any computer has been dubbed 'cloud computing'. The realisation that small, self-contained software packages can be accessed directly over the Web has led to the introduction of a whole new generation of personal computers, called 'netbooks'. Netbooks are inexpensive and small because they do not need as much internal memory. Sometimes they have no internal hard drive at all to store programs or information.

Cloud computing has led to a proliferation of web-based, pre-packaged computer programs. One of the first sites on the Web to use them was iGoogle. iGoogle offers a variety of specialised software programs that act like microsites and sit on your Google page as icons. These portable programs are called applications ('apps' for short) or 'widgets'. iGoogle's widgets offer everything from a clock to a calculator to sports reports to games to local concert listings to news reports. Widgets have allowed consumers, software developers, and hardware manufacturers to experience a flexible computing world where specialised software is tapped into or downloaded from anywhere.

Marketing apps

It wasn't long before product marketers caught on to the potential of apps. Fiat, for example, created an app to link its new Fiat 500 and Grande Punto cars directly to people's computers. Called 'eco:Drive', the app allows Fiat buyers to use a USB memory stick to plug into the car's telemetry system and then into a PC, to monitor the car's driving performance, in order to reduce carbon emissions. Eco:Drive analyses acceleration, gear changes, speed and so on to offer the user specific tips for improvement.

Not surprisingly, software developers have started to create management programs that allow marketers (and average consumers) to create multiple widgets and manage the marketing information generated by them. One such product is called 'Launch Pad', created by Los Angeles-based advertising agency Snowball. Another is Fuhu's 'Spinlets' program.

Fuhu is a web development company with headquarters in China and Los Angeles. Fuhu's goal is to create an integrated platform that allows users to consolidate, manage and distribute their 'digital life'. Fuhu does this through multiple linked products. Their product line-up is a good reflection of the importance of online applications as the backbone of online product convergence. Their core product is a widget production program (under the brand name Spinlets).

**Widget for Teressa Edwards'
album *Days Ahead***

Musicians have picked up on the
power of widgets to drive public
awareness of new releases and
direct album sales.

Spinlets allows users and content providers
to publish and distribute premium content
ubiquitously across the three key screens
(computers, TVs and mobile phones).

Spinlets includes a gallery for users to
search and find their favourite content and
post it to their favourite social networks or
home pages. It also includes a reporting
engine to provide detailed analysis of how
content is being viewed. In the same way
that blogs allowed average consumers to
compete with journalists, Spinlets allows
average consumers to compete with
multi-platform content providers. It is yet
another example of how digital technology
is turning individuals into media companies.

Another Fuhu product is called urFooz.
urFooz is a virtual identity card that allows
users to manage their digital materials,
consume content, play applications and
games, and share it across social networks.
urFooz is basically a personalised widget
that acts as your avatar on social networks.
But it does not just represent your likeness;
it brings with it everything you want to share
with others, in what looks like a personal
baseball card.

Spinlets and urFooz have been a hit with
the entertainment industry. The top-selling
rock band, Guns N' Roses, used three
different Spinlets to advertise the launch
of their 2008 release 'Chinese Democracy',
in conjunction with retailer Best Buy. The
three widgets garnered over 17 million views
and almost 3,000 direct album sales.

For years, prognosticators have predicted massive growth in mobile functionality and marketing. Yet mobile marketing has been very slow to develop. However, with the emergence of a new generation of highly capable smartphones, mobile marketing has now come of age.

In the US, mobile advertising is expected to grow a whopping 68.5% in 2009 to just under a billion dollars. And that is only considered to be modest growth. By 2013, Gartner Research expects the number to top $13 billion (£8.6 billion). That's a growth rate over four years of over 1,000%! In part, mobile's fantastic growth will be fuelled by its convergence with the other fast-growing interactive platform: social media. It was no coincidence that on a single day in 2009, Research in Motion, the maker of the Blackberry, launched <myblackberry.com>, a new online community for its users, and Facebook signed an agreement to work with mobile development company, DeviceAnywhere.

The emergence of mobile phones as a true interactive platform is leading to a broad convergence between computers and mobile phones. On the most basic level, consumers worldwide will have access to their favourite websites whenever and wherever they want to see them. In the foreseeable future, the time may arrive when people use mobile devices more than anything else for all the significant communications touch points in their lives.

SMS text marketing

One of the first and still most common forms of mobile marketing is SMS text messaging. Because text messaging requires consumers to 'opt in', it is also one of the most effective. A recent study showed that texting generates higher response rates than Internet display ads: two to ten times higher.[2]

In the US, for example, the penetration of text messaging is currently twice that of mobile Internet. In fact, in a given month, text messaging can actually outstrip mobile phone calls. For marketers, the great appeal is one of reach: consumers do not need a web-enabled smartphone to receive messages. Another appeal is simplicity. Text is considered, by many media buyers, one of the first steps in mobile marketing.

Text messaging is a tricky business, though. Regardless of its opt-in nature, messages that are not well targeted have the potential to be seen as spam. For that reason, legislation has been introduced to curb unsolicited text messages in some countries, and marketers have been wary about the potential impact of text messaging on their relationships with consumers. A mobile communications process attractive enough to entice consumers to actually 'pull' marketing information would be superior. Mobile applications are now making that a reality.

Principles of great mobile websites

The first step for most marketers is to create a great mobile website. <mobithinking.com> offers marketers ten key principles for mobile websites:

1
You need to have one
If you don't, you are missing millions of potential customers.

2
Make sure it actually works
Mobile websites work differently from computer websites. It is critical to get the functionality right.

3
Solve a real problem
Utility is the engine of the mobile web. It is not enough just to be there.

4
Maintain a laser focus
Extraneous content won't cut it on such a small screen.

5
Content is king, but in small bites
A small screen means that 'snackability' is prized.

6
Simplify, but don't over-simplify
'Small bites' doesn't mean 'bare bones'.

7
Make your site findable
Have the right naming conventions (i.e. use .mobi); make sure your .com site detects and redirects mobile users; make sure search engines pick up your .mobi site.

8
Make your site device aware
Serve the correct content for the right handset.

9
Remember the user's details
This speeds up the user's next experience.

10
Break free from .com thinking
It's still the Web, but mobile is different.

< Cloud computing and widgets
Mobile phone marketing
> Case study: ESPN's online and mobile programming

Mobile apps

The superb functionality of apps and widgets, as described earlier for the computer space, has perhaps had its greatest impact when applied to the mobile space. With the introduction of apps to the mobile space, the idea of just having a mobile website has become a starting point for marketers. The question has now become: how else can marketers add value for consumers in the mobile space, above and beyond their mobile website? If one of the golden rules for a great mobile website is to 'solve a real problem', then mobile apps allow marketers to solve dozens or even hundreds of real problems.

Mobile applications have become so popular that there are now an estimated 70,000 of them available. Alan Warms, CEO of the app review site Appolicious, and former general manager of Yahoo! News, believes that there will eventually be over one million apps available. As he puts it, 'Every company in the world is going to want one.'

Guinness' rugby mobile application

A great example of a brand adding value through a mobile phone app is Guinness. A sponsor of Hong Kong's premier sporting event, the Hong Kong Rugby Sevens, Guinness created an app for the 20,000 overseas fans attending the event. The mobile app included maps, game schedules, emergency numbers, and a translation application that would speak Cantonese (a notoriously difficult language – trust me, my wife is Cantonese). If you held up the phone and pressed the speaker button, the app could tell your cab driver to take you to a certain bar, or ask someone on the street to direct you to the nearest ATM. It was even loaded with pick-up lines such as, 'You're as beautiful as a Guinness.' Now that is solving some problems! The campaign won the Mobile Marketing Association (MMA) award for best use of mobile marketing.

The iPhone

Ground zero for the mobile app revolution has been the iconic smartphone from Apple: the iPhone. Inspired by the flexibility of widgets in the computer space, Apple created a phone whose main purpose was to act as a base for mobile applications. Soon after the phone's launch, Apple opened the iPhone App Store with a veritable library of fun and useful applications.

Early on, Apple made a brave decision in developing their apps, a decision that acted as a catalyst to unlock the latent potential of mobile phones. They decided to open up development of iPhone applications to all software developers who could meet their functionality and quality standards. This led to a swift proliferation of applications for the iPhone that made the phone far more flexible and functional than it would have been if Apple had tried to control all software development internally. New iPhone applications were developed at such a fast and furious pace, competitors were in awe.

At the end of 2009, Apple reported that they had over 15,000 apps in their App Store. To date, they have delivered over half a billion app downloads. The iPhone is currently the hottest product in mobile phones. By the end of 2008, Apple had sold over 17 million globally, over 11 million of those in just the last six months of that year.[3] By early 2010, they had sold more than 40 million units! The huge popularity of the iPhone has also fuelled big growth in similar smartphones produced by other manufacturers.

Ironically, in the US, iPhone's popularity comes amidst complaints that its basic product – telephone service, provided exclusively by AT&T – is spotty. This is in part because of the unexpected avalanche of iPhone usage on the system. In an effort to manage its reputation and explain why the network had faltered, AT&T ran a video on YouTube featuring a spokesman. According to *Advertising Age*, instead of generating goodwill and understanding, the video was seen by customers and social-media experts as being 'too little, too late'. Regardless of the performance of its phone network, however, the iPhone continues to be a gigantic hit with customers.

Target, the US retail chain, launched an iPhone app to help people find Christmas gifts. Simply enter the age, sex and personality of the person you need to buy for, along with a price range, and then shake your phone like a snow globe. Voila! You find your gift. Starbucks has even tied iPhone apps to mobile payment. One of their apps allows people to check their Starbucks card balance and reload it using a credit card. They've also tested an app that lets people pay by swiping an on-screen barcode across the store scanner.

Not to be outdone by product marketers, Internet media companies have also created useful iPhone apps. Yahoo!, for example, has created apps for some of its most popular properties, including Yahoo! Fantasy Football, Yahoo! Finance and Flickr.

〈 Cloud computing and widgets
Mobile phone marketing
〉Case study: ESPN's online and mobile programming

Real-time information

Even news reporting has tapped into the power of the iPhone. The Fwix news service, which focuses on 'hyperlocal' news, has an iPhone app that allows users to act as local reporters, uploading stories as they happen. Darien Shirazi, Fwix's 22-year-old founder, believes that the app helps to make his network a 'real-time local newswire'.

iPhone doesn't have a monopoly on apps, however. In Singapore, the alcoholic beverage brand Johnnie Walker created an app for Nokia-compatible phones. It publicises events in local bars, offers promotions and even helps users to book a cab to get them home. It is just the sort of app that you would expect from a brand that asks people to 'drink responsibly'.

We think that apps are here to stay, and that smart brands will learn how to use them strategically, recognising their potential and investing appropriately in driving adaption. We should all remember that this is a land grab for the hugely valuable real estate that is my home page or my iPhone screen.

Simon Andrews
Chief Digital Strategy Officer
MindShare

Kraft's money-making app

Savvy marketers have already figured out how to successfully blend marketing, apps and mobility. Kraft Foods, for example, has hit gold in the mobile apps game. They have created the 'iFood Assistant'. The app features over 7,000 recipes with lots of functionality, including videos, cooking tips, ingredient lists (including Kraft products) and shopping lists. Better yet for Kraft, people who download the application in the US pay 99 cents for it. Kraft's marketing application is so useful and valuable to consumers that they actually pay to receive it! Even at a price, the iFood Assistant is one of Apple's top 20 lifestyle apps. Kraft's director of innovation, Ed Kaczmarek, calls it a 'natural evolution from product to service'.

It is not surprising that Kraft is a leader in mobile marketing. They have truly embraced mobile technology. More than 4,500 Kraft employees own iPhones that were partly subsidised by the company. During the workday, employees share iPhone best practices and favourite applications.

The Android

There is also increasing excitement about the 'Android' operating system, which was first acquired by Google and later developed by the Open Handset Alliance (a group that combines Google with many of the top mobile-phone providers and handset manufacturers). Android has provided iPhone's competitors with a sophisticated open platform of their own. Motorola, for example, has introduced its 'Cliq' smartphone on the Android platform to try to revive its once dominant phone business. Not to be outdone by itself, Google announced the launch of their own Google-branded smartphone, the NexusOne, which is sold directly to consumers. Greater competition will mean faster innovation, more mobile applications and lower prices for users. Driven by the popularity of mobile applications and increased competition, the value of the global smartphone business is expected to top $200 billion (£132 billion) by 2012.[4]

Mobile video

Online viewing of video has increased significantly, and this trend has extended itself to mobile phones, which have become a true 'third screen'. In the US, for example, mobile video viewing grew over 50% in 2009, according to Nielsen's *Three Screen* report. The report notes, 'Much of this growth continues to come from increased mobile content and the rise of the mobile web as a viewing option.'

The growth of mobile video is an indication that consumers are increasingly comfortable with viewing video content on 'the best screen available'. As their comfort grows, future growth will likely make 2009's increase of 50% look very small in comparison.

〈 Cloud computing and widgets
Mobile phone marketing
〉Case study: ESPN's online and mobile programming

Mobile search

Mobile is beginning to challenge the computer in all digital marketing areas. As we learned in Chapter 2, the most profitable online advertising vehicle is search advertising. And mobile has a lot to offer there too.

A good example is a recent mobile search campaign for <Vegas.com>. In conjunction with Google, <Vegas.com> created a mobile search campaign for both the iPhone and Android platforms. The campaign has seen click-though rates that have sometimes surpassed their Internet campaigns, with click-throughs as high as 20%.

This is the first high-end iPhone campaign we have run. We are 100% satisfied with what we see, so far, in terms of iPhone search ads meeting our ROI goals, and we are likely to launch others in the future.

Scarlett Lento
Internet Marketing Manager
<Vegas.com>

Future possibilities for mobile

Large swathes of the world still have limited or no connection to telephone lines or the Internet. This communications infrastructure gap between developed and developing areas is often called the *digital divide*. However, many developing communities are starting to connect to the Internet not through computers, but through mobile phones. In places like India, where well over 50% of the population live in rural villages, over 70 million new mobile phones are being connected every year. A recent report notes that consumer-goods brands are likely to triple their online spending in India from 2009 to 2010. Growth in mobile marketing could eventually dwarf that percentage growth.

According to Ranjan Kapur, India's country manager for the global advertising agency group WPP, mobile devices can do much more than bridge the digital-access divide. There are also issues of language and literacy that create digital divides too. India has over 800 known dialects. Kapur notes that mobile phones have the potential to create a 'spoken web', which among other things could offer real-time translation services, 'enabling communications and commerce between dialects and languages'. Another opportunity he mentions is the development of a 'visual icon language that allows the rural community to interact through those visual icons to conduct commerce, conduct business, find enterprise solutions, and communicate with other people'.[5] Such advances may also help people with various linguistic disabilities worldwide. Mobile communications holds all kinds of promise.

Mobile screens and SiSoMo

Mobile marketing's future also includes its potential as a complementary medium that helps to integrate all forms of messaging. Gartner research predicts that mobile will increasingly function as a 'universal back channel' for all media, particularly in interaction with out-of-home advertising.

A few years ago, Kevin Roberts, CEO of the global advertising agency Saatchi & Saatchi, published a book entitled *SiSoMo: The Future on Screen*. The book predicted that consumers would come to stop thinking about television, computers, and mobile phones – among other hardware like game consoles and outdoor boards – as separate devices with different functionality. Instead, convergence will blur the lines between these devices. Consumers will increasingly see them simply as 'screens' of varying size and portability.

These screens share three combined elements that have always appealed to our senses: sight, sound and motion (SiSoMo for short). Roberts' book focused on sight, sound and motion, but he also believes that marketers and manufacturers of these devices will come to realise the importance of touch, and even smell, in the future. He has often said, 'What does your brand smell like? If you don't know, you should!'

The mobile platform is clearly establishing itself as a superior bridge for the digital divide.

IBM Global Innovation Outlook 3.0 Report: The New, New Media

Ultimately, Roberts believes SiSoMo is about storytelling. The convergence of technology combined with the proliferation of screen sizes and functions has opened up new creative possibilities for storytelling. Where once the 30-second commercial was the pre-eminent storytelling form, new screens and modern technology have now made almost any length or format of message viable.

The important thing is that it engages our emotions. For example, Roberts' agency launched the Toyota Yaris using a series of humorous ten-second animated ads for mobile phones. The ads – or 'mobisodes' as they called them – were short, funny and very effective. They were commercials that probably would not have worked as well on any other screen.

The new screens also increase connectivity. Screens connected to other screens that connect to the palm of our hand bring our digital life under control and help us to connect seamlessly with the digital lives of others.

Background

All-sports network ESPN is a prime example of how a broadcast channel can succeed by offering top-notch online and mobile programming, and value-added applications. ESPN recognised early on that passionate sports fans want to keep abreast of breaking sports news and scores all day long, not just when they can get to the TV. Not surprisingly, ESPN has built a powerhouse website, offering scores, live game tracking, columns, videos, fantasy leagues and the ability to personalise the site to each consumer's sports interests. <ESPN.com> is a go-to sports destination on the Web.

If having a web presence is vital for an audience that wants real-time information, news and scores, then having a strong mobile presence may be even more important. The desire to keep up with 'the game' doesn't end when you walk away from your PC.

In 2006, ESPN took a huge step. Rather than just developing mobile content, ESPN became its own mobile-phone provider. It leased its own wireless spectrum and delivered programming directly to customers on ESPN-branded phones. Their thinking was that many sports fans are obsessive and would relish a phone whose primary function was to deliver an immersive sports experience via pre-loaded software.

ESPN learned very quickly, however, that they had over-reached. Despite investing $150 million (£100 million), sources said that they signed up less than 30,000 customers, against a breakeven of 500,000. ESPN had over-estimated the average sports fan's passion for sports to the exclusion of all else. As *BusinessWeek* put it, 'As passionate as sports nuts are, they have other interests and passions… people want to be able to access more than sports on a cell phone.' That the handset was 'chunky and unremarkable' didn't help either. As one phone owner commented: 'It's like having a Lexus without the engine.'

ESPN Mobile TV
After a rocky start in the mobile space, ESPN has created a suite of mobile products that is second to none.

< Mobile phone marketing
Case study: ESPN's online and mobile programming
> Questions and exercises

Providing content

Since then, ESPN has learned their lesson. They are now out of the phone business. Their new model is to provide content to mobile phones through existing carriers. Under these new agreements, ESPN has begun to shine again as one of the most successful leaders in mobile content and application development.

One example of ESPN's mobile success is its mobile website. <ESPN.mobi> is among the top ten most visited US mobile sites. At times it gets more traffic than the .com site! <mobithinking.com> cited <ESPN.mobi> as the best working mobile site for 2008.

Another example of ESPN's success is the plethora of mobile phone apps that they make available to their fans. They offer mobile sports games, like ESPN darts and poker, ESPN ScoreCenter for scores from over 500 sports leagues around the world, and ESPN MVP to manage ESPN Fantasy League teams.

ESPN Mobile TV

Another advancement is the launch of ESPN Mobile TV, which allows viewers to watch live games on V CAST-capable phones. Television sports has come to the mobile platform with all its sight, sound and motion, if not its screen size.

ESPN Mobile is a deep product offering with mobile web, mobile video, mobile television, mobile applications, mobile games and mobile alerts. It claims to have more than eight million unique users every month, or over 60% of the US mobile web sports audience.

The story of ESPN's mobile development, which resulted in an outstanding mobile site, broadcast features and applications, is an abject lesson to all marketers: perseverance pays off. ESPN had to get it all wrong before they were able to get it all right.

> Free and supported mobile TV will help accelerate growth in the mobile TV space, and in the near future you'll see more people watching mobile TV.
>
> John Zehr
> Senior Vice President
> ESPN

ESPN's mobile content

ESPN now provides a vast amount of content through existing mobile phone networks allowing people to check the latest scores and even watch live games.

Question 1

Was ESPN's short-lived venture as an actual mobile phone provider a bad idea or did they just execute it badly?

Question 2

If you were a competing sports channel, what type of applications might you develop to get the edge on ESPN?

Question 3

What does ESPN tell us about the future of television?

Questions and exercises

Discussion questions

1

If you use applications that are readily available on the Web, how many programs that you currently have on your computer could you do without? How much memory?

2

If you were starting a new health-food supermarket, what kind of applications might you develop for the Web? For mobile?

3

Imagine that you are launching a new product into a fast-growing, culturally diverse, and language diverse market like India. What would your mobile strategy be? Are there any marketing problems mobile can solve uniquely?

Exercises

1

Visit <iGoogle.com> and create your own personalised home page. Which widgets did you choose and why? Could those widgets replace any existing software on your computer, like its built-in clock or calculator?

2

Visit the website of your favourite brand, then try to access that site using a mobile phone. Is the mobile site specifically designed for the mobile space? What does it do better or worse than the online site?

3

Watch a video on a video-enabled smartphone; discuss how the experience is different from watching on a computer screen or a TV screen. Does this make mobile video better for some types of messages and worse for others?

4

Talk to a few local restaurant managers. Ask them if search is important for their business. If so, ask them if they see any specific advantages to mobile search.

Summary

The emergence of cloud computing has begun to change how information is stored online. It has also led to the emergence of small, useful marketing programs, called 'widgets' or 'apps', that connect to the World Wide Web, providing everything from branded shopping assistants to branded translation services to branded cooking recipes. Apps have also begun to transform mobile marketing. They have helped mobile devices, such as the iPhone and Android smartphones, to realise their potential as marketing platforms. Mobile marketing has truly come of age.

Suggested further reading

Dushinski, K. 2009. *The Mobile Marketing Handbook: A Step-by-Step Guide to Creating Dynamic Mobile Marketing Campaigns*. New Jersey: CyberAge Books

Fling, B. 2009. *Mobile Design and Development: Practical Concepts and Techniques for Creating Mobile Sites and Web Apps.* California: O'Reilly Media, Inc.

Clark, J. *Best iPhone Apps: The Guide for Discriminating Downloaders.* California: O'Reilly Media, Inc.

Endnotes

1
<www.mobithinking.com>. 'The best and worst of the mobile web'. Retrieved from <www.mobithinking.com> (9 November 2009)

2
Optus Research

3
Retrieved from <www.poweredbysteam.com> (15 October 2009)

4
Cellular-News. 'Gartner sees smartphone sales worth $200 billion in 2012'. Retrieved from <www.cellular-news.com> (10 April 2010)

5
International Business Machines Corporation (2007). 'The new, new media: a global Innovation outlook 3.0 report'. New York: IBM Corporation

As we have seen in the previous chapters, the growth of online marketing is exciting in both the breadth and speed of its development. For marketing professionals, it is perhaps most exciting for its ability to generate a continuous stream of data that can be used to analyse consumer behaviour and measure return on investment (ROI).

In this chapter, we will look at some of the ways successful marketers take what could otherwise be an overwhelming amount of information and turn it into something useful for business decision making. We will also look at how the data rolls up into broader econometric models that help marketers decide which online and offline media to spend money on, and in what proportion.

This chapter is one of the shortest in this book. This is not because measurement and analytics is unimportant. Rather, as we will see, the best way to use measurement and analytics is to make sure that they are short, sharp and focused.

Online advertising offers marketers a huge range of data
Online advertising promises a new level of accountability due to its unparalleled capability to collect data. Marketers are now trying to perfect ways of analysing that data to make it useful for both companies and consumers.

<

From its earliest stages, the Internet has held the promise of being the most measurable and perhaps accountable marketing medium. Every single action a consumer takes online with your website, search ads, display ads and so on, can be measured and made to fit into models for analysis and improvement. However, this veritable feast of information can be a problem as marketers try to sift through mountains of data to find what is really important. Trying to analyse all the data, or even most of it, can lead to organisational paralysis: there is so much information and counter-information that decisions are not made easier but harder. Unnecessary data creates distracting 'noise'.

Most marketers know intuitively that excess data – data that does not make decision-making easier – is counter-productive. We will focus in this chapter on measurement processes that reduce noise and improve the ability of marketing organisations to make sound decisions. With the right measurement and analytics processes, online marketing may indeed live up to its full promise, giving it a long-term edge over other media marketing.

KPIs and dashboards

All web analytics begin by aligning your corporate and/or marketing goals directly to what you are going to measure on the Web. If you have clear marketing objectives and strategies, it will become much easier to focus on the web measures that are important. Therefore, alignment is job number one. By *alignment*, we mean having a line of sight from corporate goals to marketing goals and from marketing goals to online measures.

Measures that are in direct alignment with your objectives are called **key performance indicators (KPIs)**. KPIs are further simplified by putting them all in one report, which ideally fits on one page. It is okay to have more detail or back-up data on appendix pages, but all the basic measures you need to make decisions about the success or failure of your online marketing efforts should be shown side by side on one page.

Looking at this page is akin to driving a car. Therefore, it is commonly called a dashboard. In your car, all the key information is right there in front of you on your dashboard (things like speed, rpm, mileage, temperature, warning lights and oil pressure). Likewise, your online marketing dashboard might include such measures as click-throughs, conversion, cost per conversion, site satisfaction, or site abandonment (the percentage of people who leave your site prior to conversion).

Simplicity is prized. Dashboards should ideally never exceed ten KPI measures. Picking ten key measures out of a pile of data is never easy, but the best marketers find a way to do it. The benefit is focus.

Dashboards work best when they can be read quickly, like the dashboard on a car. Therefore, the ability to make them graphic and visually stimulating is crucial. Web companies like Google and Yahoo! both provide web analytics tools that create nice, simple, graphic dashboards for companies and consumers alike.

Google has even extended analytics to YouTube. It has combined its *Content ID* product – which allows content owners to locate, protect and make money from their copyrighted content on the Web – with *YouTube Insights*, their free analytics tool. Together, they help companies like music labels, advertisers and music studios to generate more revenue from data related to their content, which in turn should improve YouTube's profits.

SIM scoring

Social media is one of the newest areas of online marketing, and perhaps one of the hardest to figure out in terms of what measures, or KPIs, to track. The online agency, Razorfish, has tried to help remedy this with their social influence marketing (SIM) score. Developed in conjunction with TNS Cymfony/Keller Fay Group, the score looks at a brand's reach and likability based on how it is being discussed on social media sites, like Facebook and Myspace, as well as offline word of mouth. It divides measured net sentiment for the brand by measured net sentiment for the industry group. This is equal to positive plus neutral conversations about your brand minus negative conversations divided by total conversations. It is a terrific measure that can be tracked over time across brands and campaigns.

Running glossary

key performance indicators (KPIs)
the most important measures for judging business success. They are aligned with overall business objectives and should be fewer than ten in number

Top performance metrics

The Search Engine Marketing Professional Organisation (SEMPO) asked search engine marketing agencies and advertisers what metrics (KPIs) they tracked for search engine marketing programs. The results were:

- Increased traffic volume
- Conversion rate
- Click-through rate
- Return on investment
- Cost per click
- Cost per action or acquisition
- Cost of generating sales offline
- Total number of online sales
- Overall revenue increase
- Return on ad-spend
- Rank of link on search engine
- Boss satisfaction
- Brand impact[1]

Google Analytics dashboard
Having a simple, graphic dashboard with ten or fewer KPIs is a good place to start for effective online marketing analytics.

〈 A wealth of riches or information overload?
Making analytics actionable
〉 Problems with online measurement

It is one thing to have a dashboard, it is quite another to make it truly actionable. One of the best known experts on web analytics is Google's analytics evangelist, Avinash Kaushik. In his two seminal books, *Web Analytics: An Hour a Day*, and *Web Analytics 2.0*, he has done as much as anyone to make the complicated task of web analytics simple and focused. Kaushik recommends three basic steps to making web analytics actionable.

Step 1
Leverage benchmarks and goals

Measures are useless unless they are in some level of context. It is important to have a benchmark in order to gauge whether the number represents a good result or a bad one. It is also good to have a goal, so we can see if we are getting where we want to go. Context also means showing trends.

If you are doing your first web marketing campaign, and have no benchmarks, look for internal benchmarks from elsewhere in your company (if possible) or for external benchmarks, like the American Customer Satisfaction Index (ACSI), which presents satisfaction scores and rankings online for most industries.

Step 2
Create high-impact executive dashboards

This is about fine-tuning your dashboard for senior management. Your marketing dashboard may be aligned to your marketing goals, but to get top management to take notice, and make the right decisions to support marketing, you need one that is directly aligned to the CEO's corporate goals.

Trending is critical here. Top management needs to know if the numbers represent consistent progress or ebbs and flows. Are there decisions they can make to turn more ebbs into flows? Dashboards that speak their language and align with their goals will get management to help drive your agenda, which in turn will drive theirs.

Step 3
Use best practices

Some important best practices are:

■ Embrace 'churn' – online dashboards are dynamic, not static: drop measures that aren't working and add new ones on an ongoing basis.

■ One metric, one owner – make each KPI somebody's job: if it isn't performing, they need to explain why, and figure out how to improve it.

■ Walk the talk – make the dashboards a way of life for everyday decision-making, not just fodder for a once-a-month meeting.

■ Measure the effectiveness of your dashboards – make sure that the voice of the consumer is heard and be critical.

Kaushik is responsible for continuous improvement in the 'Google Analytics' tool. In 2009, the tool was updated to provide 'more intelligence and less data'. As Kaushik graphically explained it, 'We're very passionate about not doing data puking, which is essentially what many tools do today.'

A final thought about making analytics actionable is that the best analytics can help people to overcome 'analytics-phobia'. Many people are put off by the thought of something that sounds like you will need to be a mathematics expert, a computer expert, or an engineer to understand. Focused KPIs, a well-developed dashboard, and a process that is all about turning analytics into action will guarantee that the amount of mathematics people need to know is minimal, while the insight gained is maximised.

Eric Peterson, author of numerous books on web analytics, posits that effective analytics is a combination of people and technology. He notes that a few years ago companies would apply analytics technologies and just expect the insights to appear; but of course they did not. Google's Kaushik has inculcated this thinking with something he calls the 10/90 rule, which states that 10% of your web analytics budget should be spent on analytics tools, while 90% should be spent on people to interpret them.

There is such an overwhelming amount of information that can be collected, it becomes increasingly difficult to discern actionable metrics and insights under the avalanche of information.

The Online Advertising Playbook
Plummer, Rappaport, Hall and Barocci

The Lexus marketing dashboard
The Lexus dashboard is an example
of an effective use of KPIs: it is
simple, focused and actionable.
It rolls up online measures into
broader marketing measures.

Lexus' marketing dashboard

Lexus has been the best-selling luxury automotive nameplate in the United States for nine consecutive years. Lexus USA is renowned for its attention to detail and continuous improvement.

Continuous improvement is in large part about the ability to measure where you are at any given time. It is about knowing where you are, where you want to be, and how to get there. It should be no surprise that a brand whose philosophy is built on incremental improvement would have a tight definition of its marketing KPIs and a simple, yet highly effective, dashboard.

As you can see opposite, the Lexus dashboard is simple, focused and actionable. It centres on seven marketing metrics or KPIs (detailed by 13 specific measures).

It reports the results from both online and offline media efforts, including customer sales intentions, online brand buzz (i.e. engagement and word of mouth), and consumer advocacy for the brand. It effectively uses trends, goals and benchmarks to provide context for Lexus' performance on each KPI, every single month. The Lexus dashboard allows Lexus managers to see, simply and clearly, what is working and where corrective action needs to take place. This one-page document packs some real management punch.

As online marketing efforts continue to become mainstream, more companies are beginning to roll up their online dashboards into broader marketing dashboards, as Lexus has done here.

Problems with online measurement

On the surface, online marketing seems to be perfectly suited to measurement and analytics, because website log-files seem to capture every piece of information. As we have already seen, however, too much information can lead to overload. Another limitation is that website log-files do not successfully capture information about Internet users as a whole, not even their population size. This basic flaw is perhaps best explained by Fernando Bermejo from the Universidad Rey Juan Carlos in Madrid, Spain:

'Log-file analysis cannot offer a general vision of the medium because only those websites that voluntarily collaborate with the measurement process are included in the results…. To this we need to add that the quantity of information generated by the log-files is often larger than the information stored in the websites themselves. Its analysis is a complex and fastidious process… and this makes it impossible to audit all the websites online, not even all the relevant websites in a particular category.' (Barmejo: *The Internet Audience*, 2007)

Yet again, the depth of information captured on the Web is both a blessing and a curse.

The Web's limitations for measuring total Internet populations result in the ironic situation whereby traditional offline surveys are often necessary to measure online behaviour. Mixed methods, such as 'electronic measurement panels', have also been developed, using both traditional surveys and online measurement. Mixed methods collect information using traditional surveys and then select a sample of users who install measurement software in their computers for tracking. They are used as representative samples, much as the Nielson Company puts TV measurement equipment in people's homes to project national TV ratings.

There's an old quote in advertising...
'I know half my advertising is wasted;
I'm just not sure which half.' In our own
research based on careful quantitative
analysis, we found the actual waste
is about one-third.

Rex Briggs and Greg Stuart

Econometrics and marketing mix modelling

Marketing econometrics is where marketing and economic theories are combined with statistical analysis to test market relationships, such as the relationship between media mix choices and sales. An advantage of the Internet's stream of information is that it aids significantly in creating econometric media models for advertisers and marketers. The goal is to take all available media research information and combine it to create a holistic view, which will help marketers make good, profitable media decisions. And when it comes to generating statistics to be analysed, as we have seen, the online space is second to none.

As with our ROI discussions in earlier chapters (see page 60), econometric media mix models are about increased accountability for a marketing discipline (such as advertising) that has previously lacked strong fundamental principles for accountability. Remember John Wanamaker's remark: 'Half the money I spend on advertising is wasted; the trouble is I don't know which half.'

Background

In 2006, Rex Briggs and Greg Stuart released a groundbreaking book entitled *What Sticks: Why Most Advertising Fails and How to Guarantee Yours Succeeds*. In it they integrated econometric approaches into a system for advertising accountability. They called the system the communications optimisation process (or COP). Using the system properly acts like a cop (get it?) during the process, to make sure that the right decisions are being made along the way. Optimisation was defined, not surprisingly, as 'achieving the highest return on investment'.

Briggs and Stuart conducted research with over 30 top companies. Their work for Unilever's Dove beauty products brand, for example, showed that mixing media was largely about measuring the points of diminishing returns for each medium used, comparing it to their relative costs, and combining them in the most effective way. It is important to note that the point of diminishing returns in each medium is not an absolute, but rather, is relative to the product and the message.

Briggs and Stuart looked at Dove's existing media plan, which consisted of television, print and online media. Dove was very clear on the metric that defined ROI success: their advertising had to drive *purchase intent*.

Gauging effectiveness

In order to judge the effectiveness of each medium, they mapped increases of purchase intent against the number of exposures in each medium, to observe the points of diminishing return for each medium.

They then compared this information to the cost per impact of each medium. Mapping cost to effectiveness is critical because it is the only way to judge the relative efficiency of each medium.

In the words of Briggs and Stuart, 'knowing what the actual cost effectiveness of your brand is at different frequency levels for each medium is critical. There is no way you can optimise your plan without that information.'

The analysis showed that Dove's results were good, but that they still had room for improvement. They found that by trimming Dove's television and print frequency only slightly, they could increase their online reach significantly (note: because TV and print media are significantly more expensive, small cuts in these media led to big increases in online spend).

The end result: these changes would increase Dove's overall purchase intent by 14%! The cost of the research: $250,000 (£165,000). The additional revenue: millions.

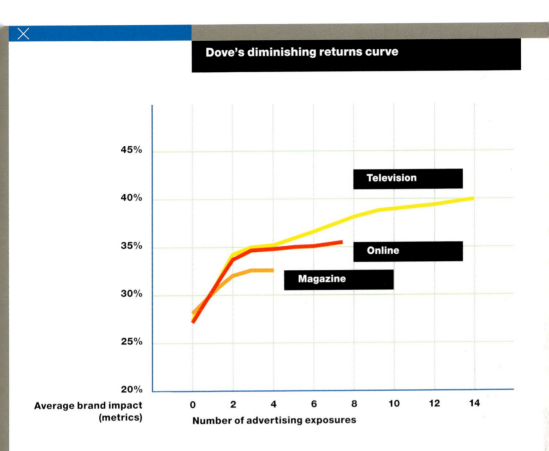

Dove's diminishing returns curve

Television

Online

Magazine

Average brand impact (metrics)

Number of advertising exposures

Dove's diminishing returns curve
Stuart and Briggs' work with Dove showed that Dove's message in each medium had a point of diminishing return, and that there was an optimum mix to maximise ROI.

< Problems with online measurement
Case study: Dove and the communications optimisation process
> Questions and exercises

✕

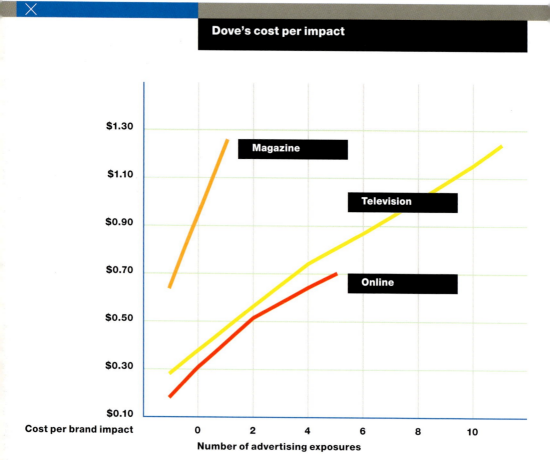

Dove's cost per impact

Cost per brand impact

Number of advertising exposures

Magazine

Television

Online

Dove's cost per impact
Mapping cost effectiveness is critical for judging actual media efficiency.

Question 1
The media analysis for Dove was conducted in 2006. How do you think the cost per impact of each of the three media used by Dove (such as TV, print and online media) have changed since then?

Question 2
What types of products or advertising messages do you think would take longer to reach a point of diminishing returns than Dove?

Question 3
Why do you think different advertising messages have different points of diminishing return?

Questions and exercises

Discussion questions

1

Is it true that you cannot manage what you cannot measure?

2

If more than ten KPIs is too much for one dashboard, how many is too few? What is a minimum number that you would need to work with to get a picture of your performance? Which ones would they be?

3

Is Kaushik's 10/90 rule the correct split between analysis tools and people to interpret them? Is there a downside to potentially having too many people to interpret them?

Exercises

1

Pick a company that intrigues you. Based on what you know about the company (and what you can find out about them) create a marketing dashboard for them. What should be their KPIs? How should their online measures be represented within their broader marketing measures?

2

Imagine that you are running a sporting goods company that sells most of its merchandise online. Make a list of the top five KPIs you would want to measure from the list of the most tracked measures reported by SEMPO (see list on page 142).

Summary

One of the greatest advantages to online marketing is the ability to collect data, analyse that data, and measure return on investment (ROI). However, a key problem is that the huge amount of data that can now be collected can be overwhelming to marketers. Trying to analyse all of it can lead to what has been termed 'paralysis by analysis'. A key to managing all this information is for marketers to focus on a handful of key performance indicators (KPIs) that drive their business. The KPI measures are incorporated in a simple (often one page), graphic, and actionable summary report called a dashboard. Analytics can also be used to create models that help marketers to figure out how best to split their marketing budget between media, and when to switch from one medium to another.

Suggested further reading

Kaushik, A. 2010. *Web Analytics: The Art of Online Accountability & Science of Customer Centricity.* Indianapolis: Wiley Publishing, Inc.

Kaushik, A. 2007. *Web Analytics: An Hour a Day.* Indianapolis: Wiley Publishing, Inc.

Bermejo, F. 2007. *The Internet Audience*, Chapters 6–8: Measurement Methods. New York: Peter Lang Publishing, Inc.

Briggs, R. and Stuart, G. 2006. *What Sticks: Why Most Advertising Fails and How to Guarantee Yours Succeeds.* Chicago: Kaplan Publishing, 2006

Endnote

1
Advertising Age

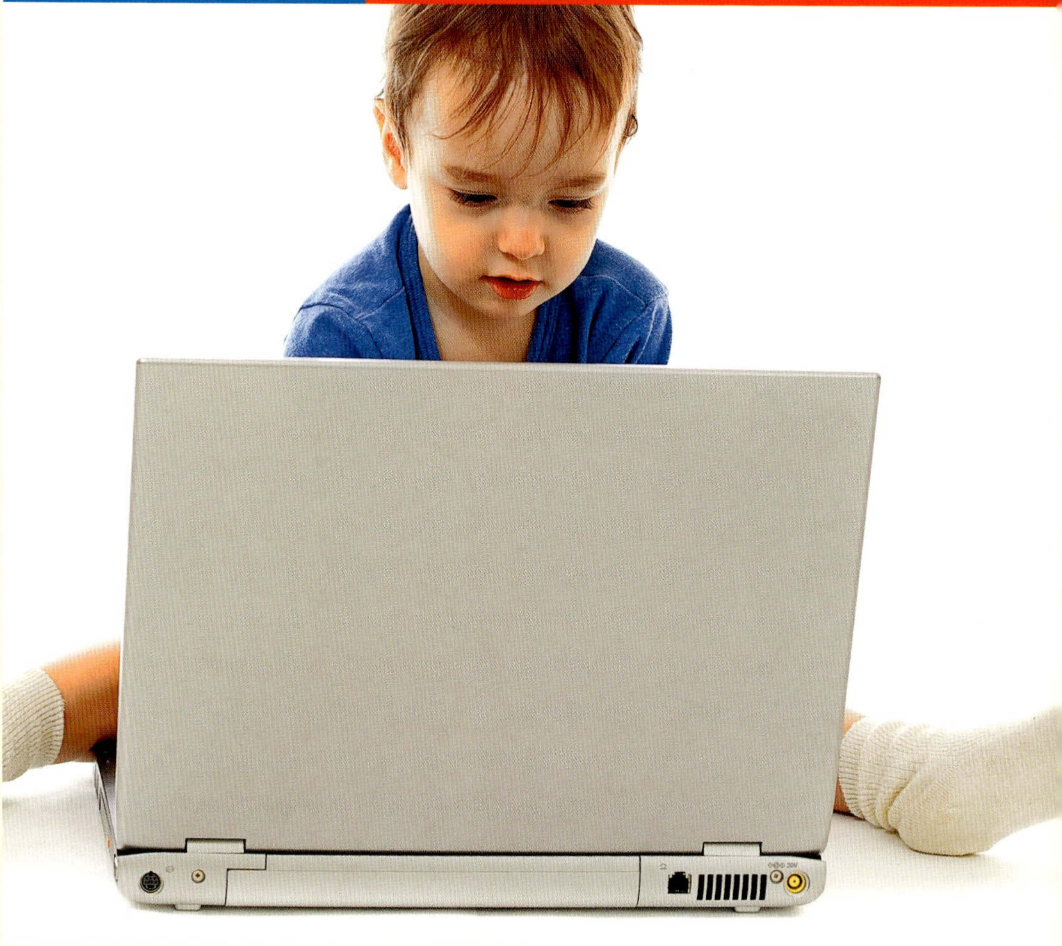

Marketing to children online presents an ethical challenge
Marketing online creates new ethical challenges for marketers, including protection of consumers' privacy, and protection of children using computers.

‹

The online environment has often been called the 'Wild West' of marketing. Marketing on the Internet has grown far more rapidly than its regulation. As such, online marketing is more susceptible to abuse and/or unethical practice than most media.

This chapter will look at the ethical issues that come into play for online marketers. We will look in detail at two specific ethical issues of which marketers need to be wary: protecting consumer privacy and online marketing to children. Both issues go right to the heart of whether a marketer can be trusted by consumers to do right by them, and to do right by society.

Protecting consumer privacy is important for all marketers, not just those who market online. However, online marketers face particular challenges because they routinely collect a significant amount of personal information, and consumers may not be aware of how much personal information is being stored or mined.

From a technical perspective, online marketers can observe the data created when you visit their websites to figure out where you live geographically, what your online preferences are, and what your online behaviour pattern looks like. They often know what sites you came from and what sites you visit next.

From a less technical perspective, online marketers often ask consumers to provide a significant amount of personal information in order for them to be able to access the most dynamic areas of their sites. If someone visits an insurance website and wants a quote, they will need to provide a significant amount of personal information to get it. All that information gets recorded and stored electronically. The same goes for automotive sites when a person wants to use the 'car configurator' tool to build a specific car. Sometimes the information is vital to the function, sometimes not. Either way, the consumer will often receive an e-mail or a phone call to follow up and try to make a sale – whether they want one or not.

Furthermore, online communication tends to involve a dialogue instead of the one-way communication of traditional media. As such, the deeper and longer the dialogue, the more the marketer knows about the consumer. Marketers use all the information they glean about individuals to profile them. This helps them to figure out which ones have the greatest sales potential. Consumers rarely think about being actively profiled or adding to a wealth of information that a company is keeping about them every time they visit a website.

How companies handle the personal information they have about consumers is an ethical issue. Just as it is always wise for e-mail marketers to let their users opt in or opt out, it is also useful for online marketers to let consumers access their personal data, preferences, and so on, and let them edit it or delete it. It is also better to ask them if they want the next step in the sales process to occur before they receive any unwanted communication.

Selling personal data

A bigger ethical dilemma for online marketers is whether to share or sell personal data. As discussed earlier in this book (see page 65), large companies with multiple brands may find that one brand's 'bad data' is another brand's 'good data'. In other words, a website visitor for one brand might fit another brand's key sales profile. Should they share the information with the other brand? Should they sell it to another company?

Many companies pay significant sums to other companies to gather data on consumers who fit their sales profiles. For example, even before the advent of online marketing, a number of financial credit companies sold personal financial information and credit scores freely without the knowledge of their own customers.

The European Commission has even started legal action against the UK government for failing to protect privacy on the Web. A behavioural targeting scheme run through some of Britain's biggest Internet service providers, by a company called Phorm, gathered information without the awareness of consumers.

As if to underscore the increased importance of privacy as it related to marketing communications, the world's largest advertising agency holding company, Omnicom, recently advertised a new position for senior counsel for privacy and regulatory matters. This makes Omnicom the second top agency holding company to create what is being referred to as a 'Privacy Tsar'.

Clearly, the best ethical position for online marketers is to make each consumer aware of the information that the company holds, give the consumer significant control over it, and never share or sell it without their knowledge. In fact, sometimes sharing and selling of information can be highly beneficial to consumers. It can get them in touch with companies and products that perfectly meet their needs. However, it is always best for the consumer, rather than the company, to decide what is in their best interests.

×

All of us who professionally use the mass media are the shapers of society. We can vulgarise that society. We can brutalise it. Or we can help lift it onto a higher level.

Bill Bernbach
Former Chairman & CEO
Doyle, Dane, Bernbach (DDB)

Facebook and the use of personal data

Facebook is the world's most popular social networking site, where millions of people share highly personal information. When Facebook created 'Beacon' to tap into people's online behaviour and share it with their network of friends and outside companies, the negative reaction was swift and loud.

Personal data 2.0

A trend we are likely to see emerge in online marketing will come from increasing consumer awareness and control of their personal data. In an idea originally put forward by Harvard professor John Deighton, instead of looking to government or industry regulators to help protect consumer privacy, consumers should capitalise on the value of their information and sell it themselves for a profit through intermediate companies. He sees this as a market solution to a vexing problem: the difference between 'privacy as a right and identity as an asset'.[1]

This may be a long way off, however. Although consumers are starting to gain awareness of the value of their personal information to companies, a successful solution is likely to require the emergence of third-party companies to broker the millions of agreements between companies and individuals.

Facebook Beacon

In November 2007, Facebook launched an advertisement system named 'Beacon'. The purpose of Beacon was to mine Facebook users' online behavioural data, from over 40 partner websites, to allow for targeted advertising. Additionally, some of the information would be shared with others on Facebook as part of the users' news feeds. As a specific example, one of the partners was the movie ticket-purchase site Fandango. So, if you bought tickets to a certain movie, both advertisers and friends would know.

Beacon created a firestorm almost from day one. Within just two weeks, the civic and political action group <moveon.org> created a Facebook group demanding that Facebook not release such personal information without permission. Within two more weeks, the group had over 50,000 members.

Beacon quickly succumbed to pressure by creating an opt-out mechanism, and Facebook founder Mark Zuckerman apologised for the mishap. According to <moveon.org> spokesman, Adam Green: 'We hope this has a ripple effect throughout the industry, and sets a precedent that it is unacceptable to assume that it's OK to share private information without permission.'

Things did not get better, however. Reports circulated that, despite the opt-outs, in some cases private information was still being collected and posted. In August 2008, a class action lawsuit was filed in the US against Facebook and their advertising partners alleging that the sharing of information without consent was in violation of numerous federal and state privacy laws.

In September 2009, Facebook announced it would be shutting down Beacon.

< Privacy
Online marketing to children
> Case study: Geppetto and responsible marketing to children

Marketing to children in any medium is fraught with ethical challenges. Numerous studies have shown that children under the ages of seven or eight rarely understand the real intent of television advertising. An experiment conducted by the University of Sheffield in England and Fordham University in the US (Ali, Blades, Oates & Blumberg, 2009) exposed web pages, including advertisements, to adults and children. While adults were 'almost perfect' in identifying the ads on the web pages, children had significant trouble distinguishing them from other content. The ten-year-olds identified about three-quarters of the ads. The eight-year-olds identified about half. The six-year-olds identified only about a quarter of the ads.

In the online environment, concerns are heightened because of the medium's unique nature, as well as issues of content and access. According to Sabrina Neeley of Miami University, Ohio – who has undertaken detailed analyses of Internet advertising and children – online communications may 'provide a unique context for communications with children because of its confluence of different media characteristics and its interactivity'.

Neeley points to a number of specific areas of concern about the unique nature of online media regarding children:

Time and attention concerns
She notes that the interactive nature of the Internet may lead children to lapse into a 'flow' state. In this almost trance-like state, children's engagement and attention are such that they may be much more susceptible to advertising suggestions.

Vulnerability to advertisers' messages and tactics
Marketing messages and tactics have become so intertwined that children have a hard time separating them. For example, most commercial sites targeted at children contain games, puzzles or contests. These games are branded and often have a direct selling intent (these are known as 'adver-games').

Differentiation between reality and fantasy
Younger children often have difficulty distinguishing between reality and fantasy when it comes to such things as animated characters. This is exacerbated in the online space by the virtual reality dimension of the Web, which makes differentiation significantly more difficult.

Neopets and two California elementary schools

Ellen Seiter, a professor at University of Southern California, who worked closely with children in two public elementary schools in southern California, experienced these issues first hand when she monitored her students' reaction to the commercial website for Neopets (a 'virtual pet community'):

'When I first looked at the Neopets site, I was stunned at the embedded advertising, and the commercial audacity of some of the schemes for gaining points. When the children in my class look at the site, they primarily see opportunities for victory, fame and fortune in a fan community.

'After some reflection on why our reactions were so different, I realised I should ask the children straight out why they thought <neopets.com> existed. To my surprise, all the students gave the same answer, more or less: Neopets was just a cool idea of a lone individual who wanted to share the fun. Neopets existed because somebody, somewhere, had made up something cool, had a good idea, and put it on the Web for our enjoyment…. When I asked if it cost money to produce Neopets, they answered no, just the cost of the computer. Their high level of involvement helped to dull their awareness of the commercialism.'[2]

Seiter sums up her research by stating that, 'the World Wide Web is a more aggressive and stealthy marketer than television ever was…'. In order to act ethically, online marketers must be conscious of its inherent stealth, and of how it dulls children's commercial awareness of every embedded message that they experience online.

< Privacy
Online marketing to children
> Case study: Geppetto and responsible marketing to children

Online junk food marketing

One category that has received particular scrutiny for ethical online behaviour towards children has been food marketers, particularly those selling snack foods, or foods with high fat or sugar content. Online media has opened up new avenues for junk food marketers to approach children in a less regulated and less expensive environment than traditional media such as television.

Recently, the Kaiser Family Foundation in the US undertook the first systematic analysis of the content of online food marketing to children. The analysis looked at over 4,000 unique web pages. The results show that children's exposure to junk food messages has proliferated beyond the ads that they see on TV:

■ 85% of leading food brands targeting children provided online content.

■ 97% of brands offering adver-games incorporated at least one brand 'marker' like a food item, product package or brand character; 80% had two or more brand markers; 64% had the brand marker as a prominent or featured part of the game.

■ 79% of sites featured some type of specific advertising statement.

■ 64% made use of viral marketing where children were encouraged to send e-mails to friends about the companies' products.

■ 53% had television commercials available for viewing, effectively making their ads visible 24 hours a day.

To be fair, 72% of brands included some type of nutritional information, but almost half of those presented nutritional information in a form that the study dubbed 'advercation': a combination of advertising and education that might present the information using a brand character, for example.

In one sense, concerns about fast-food marketing on the Web are no different from concerns about fast-food marketing to kids in general. The online tactics are perhaps less of an issue with critics than the nature of the product itself. Many companies who market to kids do so with wholesome products that are presented ethically, both online and offline.

COPPA and self-regulation

While the special nature of children's relationship to online media may be cause for concern, there are safeguards in place. In the US, legislation protects children online. The Children's Online Privacy Protection Act of 1998 (COPPA) requires commercial operators of websites to obtain 'verifiable parental consent' before collecting or disclosing personal information about children under 13 years old. The COPPA legislation has influenced many other countries, including Canada and Australia, to pass similar laws. And COPPA also applies to any foreign-owned website targeting children in the US. It is truly international in its scope and influence.

Industry self-regulation is also strong. The Children's Advertising Review Unit (CARU) of the Council of Better Business Bureaus has set out a series of data-collection rules protecting the privacy rights of children and their parents, which are followed on a voluntary basis by industry. CARU's goal is to promote truthful, accurate and appropriate advertising to children wherever it appears. According to Wayne Keeley, director of CARU and vice president of the Council of Better Business Bureaus, 'We try to find the common ground between protection of children, which is our uppermost priority, and responsible advertising'.

CARU's online guidelines were actually the basis for COPPA, which indicates that most marketers voluntarily try to approach children using ethical practice. Professional marketers realise that ethical practice is always better for business in the long run. In many cases they even become society's most effective advocates for children's rights and protection.

< Online marketing to children
Case study: Geppetto and responsible marketing to children
> Questions and exercises

Background

Marketers who want to target children are increasingly engaging with partners who understand children's special needs. These companies can balance the ethical need to protect children (respecting existing legislation and guidelines) and the need to get their message across in a way that builds brands and promotes sales growth. One such company is the youth advertising agency Geppetto.

Geppetto, named after Pinocchio's father in the iconic children's story, lists their speciality target audiences as kids, tweens, teens, young adults and, of course, parents. Their past and present client list reads like a who's who of top marketers: Coca-Cola, Nike, Dannon (Danone in UK), Levi's, McDonald's, Samsung, Intel and many more.

Geppetto's CEO, Julie Halpin Anderson, takes her job and her responsibility seriously. She states, 'Our goal is to enhance the lives of young people and their families by helping create products, and connect them to products, that make their lives better. While we do that, we need to be extremely careful not to exploit them in any way. In this age of digital media, where the consumer is increasingly in charge, we want to enable kids to take charge in their interactions with our clients. We want the kids to be in total control, and we want their moms to be comfortable that we are doing the best for their kids.'

Appealing to parents

Geppetto's rule that 'mom is there too' is important. If marketers look through a parent's eyes, it is harder to make a mistake. For example, the US accessories company Almar Sales came to Geppetto to help them engage young girls with their vast product line of dress-up accessories, clothing and room décor. Geppetto understood that many little girls go through a princess phase, and that Almar's products were the perfect way for girls to experiment and 'try on' the princess persona. The insight for Almar was that their products did not prescribe that a princess look any particular way. So, while Hollywood studios were giving little girls complete images of what a princess should be, Almar was inviting girls to discover their own princess.

To make this concept come to life, Geppetto developed a brand and a virtual place online called My Princess Academy (<myprincessacademy.com>) – the place for little girls to go and play at being a princess. To appeal to parents, the site talked about the values of generosity, intelligence, beauty and confidence as being the qualities that all true princesses have. For kids, it had age-appropriate games and activities that brought the strategic idea to life. This brand idea and virtual world gave Almar a platform for their products that had meaning and interest to both girls and their parents.

A company that enshrines its friendship for protective legislation is a company that is on the right ethical track. More companies would be well advised to follow suit.

Ethical rules

Respect the user

Young people are developing and, as a consequence, have limited abilities and capabilities to enjoy what online environments have to offer. Understand the developmental stage of your core user and develop appropriate content for that life-stage, (more pictures than words for young readers; more sophistication and levels for savvy video-game players).

Protective legislation is your friend

The COPPA legislation (the Children's Online Privacy Protection Act) was carefully crafted to both protect children *and* to provide appropriate licence and freedom to marketers who wanted to bring their brands alive for kids online. By embracing these guidelines, marketers are likely to develop sites that work and protect kids in the process.

'Mom is there too'

Just because a site is developed for kids, it is critical to remember that the child's parents are likely to be participating with their child to some degree depending on their age. Therefore, it is important to consider developing content that speaks to both.

Effectiveness rules

Be crystal clear about your objective and set reasonable, measurable metrics to assess success

Too often, marketers want a site without being clear about why they want it. Kids' expectations are extremely high and their patience is short. It's critical to be clear about what you want to accomplish so that you can track it and be straight with kids.

Early payoff

Kids are not patient and will not click through multiple screens to find something that they enjoy. Make it simple, easy and satisfying right off the bat, and they'll stick around. If it's hard, you've lost them.

Kids love the new, quirky and unexpected

But if the environment feels too unfamiliar, kids will not feel confident enough to stay and explore. A balance of familiar and surprising elements will entice and satisfy kids.

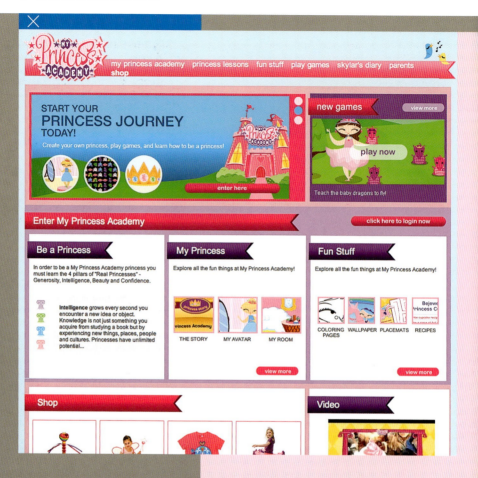

My Princess Academy website

Clients can improve their ability to run ethical work by working with agencies that specialise in specific audiences or issues. 'My Princess Academy' was created by Geppetto, an advertising agency and marketing consultancy that focuses on communicating to young people.

Question 1

Which one of Geppetto's ethical rules do you think is most important and why?

Question 2

In an effort to be an ethical marketer to children, what are the advantages to using a specialist children's advertising agency? Are there any potential drawbacks?

Questions and exercises
〉

Discussion questions

1

Is personal data still personal property after you have shared it with a company online?

2

Do you believe that consumers will ever be in a situation where they can get companies to 'bid' for their personal data online?

3

Do we need more legislation to help protect children from marketers online, or is there enough to ensure that online children's marketing does no more harm than in traditional media?

Exercises

1

Make a list of the kind of data that marketers have about you, based on your interaction with them online and offline. Which information would you not want them to share? Which information might be useful (to you) for them to share?

2

Hold a debate. One side should argue from <moveon.org>'s point of view that Beacon was overstepping the mark. The other side should argue that Beacon was adding value and not invading privacy. At the end of the debate, decide which team had the strongest arguments.

Summary

The marketing of products such as tobacco, pharmaceuticals and fast food, can pose ethical challenges. Similarly, marketing to some target audiences can also pose ethical concerns (for example, selling to children and the elderly). Online marketing can exacerbate these challenges because it is less regulated than traditional media.

Online marketing also creates new challenges concerning issues of consumer privacy, due to the vast amounts of information marketers can collect about their customers and visitors over the Web. A key to online ethics is to make consumers aware of the information the company has and to put them in control of its use. It is also important to follow the intent of protective legislation (such as COPPA), and to become an advocate for the rights and protection of the special audiences that your products serve, as we saw in Geppetto's approach to children's online marketing.

Suggested further reading

Seiter, E. 2007. *The Internet Playground: Children's Access, Entertainment and Mis-Education.* New York: Peter Lang Publishing Group

Ess, C. 2009. *Digital Media Ethics: Digital Media and Society Series.* UK: Polity Press

Endnotes

1
Cnet news, HBS Working Knowledge, 1 September, 2003

2
Seiter, E. (2007). *The Internet playground.* New York: Peter Lang Publishing Inc.

In 2001, Ray Kurzweil proposed the 'law of accelerating returns'. It posits that technological change happens exponentially rather than additively. This suggests that the digital media revolution will continue at a rate of change that is accelerating (in other words, we will see more changes in the next five years than we saw in the last ten). From a marketer's perspective, the latest news headlines seem to support this conclusion. In 2009, sales of web ads surpassed sales of TV ads in Britain. Television networks are exploring the combination of television and social networking to build the groundwork for 'Social TV', whereby viewers using Twitter feeds, for example, can become involved directly in the programmes.

In 2007, IBM Global Business Services released a booklet, entitled *The End of Advertising as We Know it*. In it they stated: 'As we have seen in previous disruptive cycles, the future cannot be extrapolated from the past…. [Therefore] it is imperative to plan for different future scenarios and build competitive capabilities for all of them.' The past does tell us, however, that the broad directions of social and technological change can be predicted with some accuracy. One such broad direction of change, which has been a constant theme in this book, is convergence. It is an ineluctable trend that will shape online marketing, and all marketing, for at least the next ten years.

My friend and mentor, Kevin Roberts, reminds us of the importance of convergence. In his book *SiSoMo: The Future on Screen*, he explains that the differences between online and offline media will continue to be minimised. In another of his books, *Lovemarks*, he explains that we need to place even more importance on creating brands that have mystery, sensuality and intimacy. We may pursue our obsession to measure ROI, and the newfound tools to do so in consummate detail. Meanwhile, the brands that can connect emotionally with consumers will win; online and offline. Emotion trumps reason every time. Always has, always will.

The essential difference between emotion and reason is that emotion leads to action while reason leads to conclusions.

Donald Caine
Neurologist

The author would like to thank the following for their help with the book:

Al Reid	Larry Elin
Amy Falkner	Lorraine Branham
Andrew Stone	Maria Fong Sheehan
Antony Young	Mark Templin
Betsy Feeley	Mark Turner
Bill Cochrane	Matt Murphy
Bob Carter	Milano Reyna
Bob Isherwood	Mitch Winkels
Bob Seelert	Nilla Sheehan
Boo Boo	Paul Mareski
Carla Hofler	Paul Silverman
Carla Lloyd	Robb Fujioka
Clare Sheehan	Ruth Slattery
Clare Slattery	Sharon Kondo
Danny Burke	Shavvah Aldred
Daria Sheehan	Sheryl Addotta
Dave Nordstrom	Tom Eslinger
David Shaw	Trudy Vitti
Deb Senior	Vin Crosby
Deborah Wahl Meyer	Vincent Tipaldo
Ed Russell	Wayne Keeley
Edythe S. Connolly	William G. Sheehan, Jr
Georgia Kennedy	William G. Sheehan, Sr
Hank Sheehan	
Jackie Ashkenazie	
James Tsao	
Janie Sheehan	
Jay Black	
Jim Mitchell	
John Lisko	
Julie Halpin	
Kate Sheehan	
Kathy Sheehan	
Kevin O'Neill	
Kevin Roberts	
Kevin Sheehan	

Index compiled by Indexing Specialists (UK) Ltd
Indexing House
306a Portland Road
Hove
East Sussex BN3 6LP
United Kingdom
Tel: +44 1273 416777
Email: indexers@indexing.co.uk
www.indexing.co.uk

BASICS
MARKETING

Working with ethics

Lynne Elvins
Naomi Goulder

Publisher's note

The subject of ethics is not new, yet its consideration within the applied visual arts is perhaps not as prevalent as it might be. Our aim here is to help a new generation of students, educators and practitioners find a methodology for structuring their thoughts and reflections in this vital area.

AVA Publishing hopes that these **Working with ethics** pages provide a platform for consideration and a flexible method for incorporating ethical concerns in the work of educators, students and professionals. Our approach consists of four parts:

The **introduction** is intended to be an accessible snapshot of the ethical landscape, both in terms of historical development and current dominant themes.

The **framework** positions ethical consideration into four areas and poses questions about the practical implications that might occur. Marking your response to each of these questions on the scale shown will allow your reactions to be further explored by comparison.

The **case study** sets out a real project and then poses some ethical questions for further consideration. This is a focus point for a debate rather than a critical analysis so there are no predetermined right or wrong answers.

A selection of **further reading** for you to consider areas of particular interest in more detail.

Ethical: awareness/ reflection/ debate

Introduction

Ethics is a complex subject that interlaces the idea of responsibilities to society with a wide range of considerations relevant to the character and happiness of the individual. It concerns virtues of compassion, loyalty and strength, but also of confidence, imagination, humour and optimism. As introduced in ancient Greek philosophy, the fundamental ethical question is: *what should I do?* How we might pursue a 'good' life not only raises moral concerns about the effects of our actions on others, but also personal concerns about our own integrity.

In modern times the most important and controversial questions in ethics have been the moral ones. With growing populations and improvements in mobility and communications, it is not surprising that considerations about how to structure our lives together on the planet should come to the forefront. For visual artists and communicators, it should be no surprise that these considerations will enter into the creative process.

Some ethical considerations are already enshrined in government laws and regulations or in professional codes of conduct. For example, plagiarism and breaches of confidentiality can be punishable offences. Legislation in various nations makes it unlawful to exclude people with disabilities from accessing information or spaces. The trade of ivory as a material has been banned in many countries. In these cases, a clear line has been drawn under what is unacceptable.

But most ethical matters remain open to debate, among experts and lay-people alike, and in the end we have to make our own choices on the basis of our own guiding principles or values. Is it more ethical to work for a charity than for a commercial company? Is it unethical to create something that others find ugly or offensive?

Specific questions such as these may lead to other questions that are more abstract. For example, is it only effects on humans (and what they care about) that are important, or might effects on the natural world require attention too?

Is promoting ethical consequences justified even when it requires ethical sacrifices along the way? Must there be a single unifying theory of ethics (such as the Utilitarian thesis that the right course of action is always the one that leads to the greatest happiness of the greatest number), or might there always be many different ethical values that pull a person in various directions?

As we enter into ethical debate and engage with these dilemmas on a personal and professional level, we may change our views or change our view of others. The real test though is whether, as we reflect on these matters, we change the way we act as well as the way we think. Socrates, the 'father' of philosophy, proposed that people will naturally do 'good' if they know what is right. But this point might only lead us to yet another question: *how do we know what is right?*

You
What are your ethical beliefs?

Central to everything you do will be your attitude to people and issues around you. For some people, their ethics are an active part of the decisions they make every day as a consumer, a voter or a working professional. Others may think about ethics very little and yet this does not automatically make them unethical. Personal beliefs, lifestyle, politics, nationality, religion, gender, class or education can all influence your ethical viewpoint.

Using the scale, where would you place yourself? What do you take into account to make your decision? Compare results with your friends or colleagues.

Your client
What are your terms?

Working relationships are central to whether ethics can be embedded into a project, and your conduct on a day-to-day basis is a demonstration of your professional ethics. The decision with the biggest impact is whom you choose to work with in the first place. Cigarette companies or arms traders are often-cited examples when talking about where a line might be drawn, but rarely are real situations so extreme. At what point might you turn down a project on ethical grounds and how much does the reality of having to earn a living affect your ability to choose?

Using the scale, where would you place a project? How does this compare to your personal ethical level?

01 02 03 04 05 06 07 08 09 10

01 02 03 04 05 06 07 08 09 10

Your specifications
What are the impacts of your materials?

In relatively recent times, we are learning that many natural materials are in short supply. At the same time, we are increasingly aware that some man-made materials can have harmful, long-term effects on people or the planet. How much do you know about the materials that you use? Do you know where they come from, how far they travel and under what conditions they are obtained? When your creation is no longer needed, will it be easy and safe to recycle? Will it disappear without a trace? Are these considerations your responsibility or are they out of your hands?

Using the scale, mark how ethical your material choices are.

Your creation
What is the purpose of your work?

Between you, your colleagues and an agreed brief, what will your creation achieve? What purpose will it have in society and will it make a positive contribution? Should your work result in more than commercial success or industry awards? Might your creation help save lives, educate, protect or inspire? Form and function are two established aspects of judging a creation, but there is little consensus on the obligations of visual artists and communicators toward society, or the role they might have in solving social or environmental problems. If you want recognition for being the creator, how responsible are you for what you create and where might that responsibility end?

Using the scale, mark how ethical the purpose of your work is.

01 02 03 04 05 06 07 08 09 10

01 02 03 04 05 06 07 08 09 10

One aspect of marketing that raises an ethical dilemma is the extent to which marketing techniques might persuade or influence consumers to purchase items that they may not need or that may even be detrimental. Central to this question is the balance of power in the relationship between the seller and the buyer. Marketers emphasise the positive attributes of a product or service and cement favourable associations in the minds of the target audience, usually to generate sales. In free markets, buyers should be able to compare and choose from a variety of competitive options. However, as marketing has become increasingly diverse in its formats and complex in its application of psychological techniques, questions can be raised about the freedom of individuals to choose fairly. Do marketers genuinely feel positive about the products and services that they help to promote, or are they driven purely to make profit for themselves and the seller? Should marketers take responsibility for ensuring that buyers can make fully informed choices? Or is this issue already taken care of through independent consumer groups and anti-trust law?

Social marketing has become increasingly popular among governments and campaign groups as a way of addressing serious health issues, particularly in developing countries. The global HIV/AIDS epidemic is stabilising, but it is still at an unacceptably high level. According to UNAIDS figures, an estimated 33 million people across the globe were living with HIV in 2007, around 22 million of whom resided in sub-Saharan Africa.

Although not the only method of prevention available, the male latex condom is the most efficient and readily available technology capable of reducing the sexual transmission of HIV and other sexually transmitted infections. In the mid 1980s, the social marketing of condoms emerged as an effective tool in the fight to combat the spread of HIV/AIDS. Programmes made condoms available, affordable and acceptable in countries affected by the epidemic and used marketing messages to raise awareness of the disease.

One marketing technique that might be deployed is to recruit prominent individuals and groups to deliver and endorse safer sex messages. This approach has been successful through the recruitment of sports and music figures, religious leaders and politicians.

In 1996, Archbishop Tutu delivered an impassioned plea for South Africans to face the facts about HIV/AIDS in a television documentary entitled 'The Rubber Revolution'. Tutu, along with other religious leaders and various national sports figures, discussed the importance of open conversations about sexuality and HIV/AIDS. Prior to Tutu's involvement, the South African Broadcasting Corporation had not allowed the word 'condom' to be used on primetime television.

With support from USAID and other non-profit organisations, the condom brand Prudence was introduced to Zaire in 1996. Previous to this campaign, the total number of condoms given away or sold in Zaire was approximately 500,000 a year. In 1999, four million Prudence condoms were sold. A key tactic in the marketing campaign was the placement and pricing strategy. By selling Prudence condoms via street hawkers at three cents each, people were able to get hold of condoms anywhere at any time. Salespeople were also supported with Prudence key rings, bartender aprons, calendars, hats and signs; and music events offered half-price admission to anyone with a Prudence pack. The marketing campaign has been so successful that Zairians now use 'Prudence' as a generic term for a condom.

Is it more ethical to practise social marketing than commercial marketing?

Is it unethical to pay somebody to endorse a product or service that they do not use?

Would you work on a project to market condoms in African countries?

There is an increasing political and social consensus that something needs to be done to safeguard children from the worst excesses of direct marketing and the pressures of commercialisation.

Reverend Dr Rowan Williams

Further reading

AIGA
Design Business and Ethics
2007, AIGA

Eaton, Marcia Muelder
Aesthetics and the Good Life
1989, Associated University Press

Ellison, David
Ethics and Aesthetics in European Modernist Literature:
From the Sublime to the Uncanny
2001, Cambridge University Press

Fenner, David E W (Ed)
Ethics and the Arts:
An Anthology
1995, Garland Reference Library of Social Science

Gini, Al and Marcoux, Alexei M
Case Studies in Business Ethics
2005, Prentice Hall

McDonough, William and Braungart, Michael
Cradle to Cradle:
Remaking the Way We Make Things
2002, North Point Press

Papanek, Victor
Design for the Real World:
Making to Measure
1972, Thames & Hudson

United Nations Global Compact
The Ten Principles
www.unglobalcompact.org/AboutTheGC/TheTenPrinciples/index.html